THE DUKE FOREST AT 75

A Resource for All Seasons

The Duke Forest at 75

A Resource for All Seasons

by Ida Phillips Lynch

OFFICE OF THE DUKE FOREST
DUKE UNIVERSITY
DURHAM, NORTH CAROLINA
2006

The Duke Forest at 75: A Resource for All Seasons
By Ida Phillips Lynch

Edited by Maura High and Judson Edeburn
Design and typesetting by Azalea Graphics

Published by the Office of the Duke Forest
Box 90332
Duke University
Durham, North Carolina 27708

First printing, October 2006
Second printing, February 2007

ISBN 0-9789646-1-6 (bound)
ISBN 0-9789646-0-8 (paperback)

5 4 3 2 1

Contents

Acknowledgements

As the year 2001 rolled around I began to think about the fact that in just five years Duke Forest would be 75 years old. Well, many of the trees in the Forest are older than that, but Duke University, under Dr. Clarence Korstian's able leadership, established the Duke Forest some 75 years ago. In announcing the establishment of the Forest, Duke University president William Few wrote in the foreword to the first issue of *Forestry Bulletin* that "Duke University has entered upon a program of educational work in forestry and is engaged in the organization and development of the Duke Forest in such a way as to make it of the largest possible educational use."

As I started mulling over a good way to celebrate this 75-year anniversary, I recalled the many old maps and records and all the individuals like Few, Korstian, Maughan, Blackmon, and White who made it all happen over the years, along with many able assistants and countless students. It seemed like it was time to get some of this rich history down on paper. As it turned out, in 2001, an incoming student to the Nicholas School of the Environment and Earth Sciences, Scott Bodien, was interested in diving into such a project. In 2002 Scott began accumulating information and interviewing folks who had, in some way, been part of the Forest's history. Over the next two years Scott and I interviewed more than 35 people, including graduates of the School, faculty, Duke administrators, staff of government agencies, neighboring landowners, and many more.

After languishing a bit, our efforts were revitalized in the summer of 2005 when, at the suggestion of Richard Broadwell, the Duke Forest program director, we brought on board Ida Phillips Lynch of Niche Publishing LLC (www.nichepress.com) to build on the research that Scott and I had begun and to write the book. Ida interviewed additional experts, and she and I reviewed an immense amount of information. Delving into the archives, old files, and photo collections has been an education in itself. The book that Ida has written based on all this research is a fascinating portrait not only of the Duke Forest but also of the history and landscape that surrounds it.

I especially appreciate the enthusiasm and information imparted by Gail Boyarsky. Her knowledge of the history of the area and interviews with Glenn and Stanford Whitfield were immensely helpful.

I want to sincerely thank Dr. Marcia Angle for her deep interest in the Forest and her financial contribution to the project, and also the Forest History Society for supporting Scott in the initiation of the project. Without their assistance the project would not have gotten under way.

The process has provided me the opportunity to meet and talk to new folks and renew old acquaintances through the many interviews and recollections we have amassed. We list below the individuals who have helped so greatly in providing facts, quotes, background and inspiration for this book. Some are cited in the pages that follow, and all are part of the story.

– Judson Edeburn,
Duke Forest Resource Manager

RESEARCHING AND WRITING THIS BOOK deepened my understanding of the history and ecology of the Piedmont landscape. Although I am a native of the region, I was unfamiliar with many of the rich stories found in the rolling hills of home. I was fortunate to meet many knowledgeable guides along the way who graciously shared their perspectives on and affection for Duke Forest.

Jean Bradley Anderson kindly shared her thoughtful insights into local and North Carolina history. Her book *Durham County* is an affectionate and engaging county history that is seamlessly intertwined with the history of North Carolina overall. David Southern graciously shared his extensive knowledge of the area and his research into land deeds and family histories and accompanied me on several walks in the Forest. Professors Norm Christensen and Dan Richter with the Nicholas School of the Environment and Earth Sciences shared their perspectives and connections to Duke Forest in several interviews. Research associate and naturalist Jeff Pippen shared his knowledge of the Forest's bird and butterfly life and the research scene.

Archaeologist Randy Daniel offered his insights into Native American history in and around Duke Forest. English professor and poet James Applewhite shared his perspectives on the Forest as a source of inspiration and allowed us to reprint one of his poems in the book. And all of them took time from their busy schedules to review and provide invaluable comments to various sections of the manuscript. I thank you all.

Thanks, too, to my husband Merrill, who walked with me in the woods throughout the seasons and helped interpret the landscape and flora and fauna, and to my sister Elizabeth, who accompanied me on some great walks in the Forest on several beautiful winter and early spring days.

Thank you also to Richard Broadwell and Bobbie Reeves of the Duke Forest staff for their great help throughout the project. And a special thanks to Judd Edeburn for overseeing the process, sharing his incredible knowledge of the Forest, and maintaining his cheerful nature in the face of many deadlines.

– Ida Phillips Lynch,
www.nichepress.com

Contributors

An extraordinary collection of people from the Duke University community, local communities, and beyond contributed their time and talents to the creation of this book. The Office of Duke Forest wishes to thank all of them for their devotion to the Duke Forest.

We thank to the staff of the following libraries and collections for their insights into the history of Duke Forest and environs: the Duke University Archives; the Rare Book, Manuscript and Special Collections Library, Duke University; and the North Carolina Collection, University of North Carolina-Chapel Hill.

The following people were interviewed or provided recollections about their thoughts and perspectives on the Forest. Although space prohibits us from incorporating all of their comments directly in the book, they provided an invaluable resource for the book, and we greatly appreciate their contribution to the project. We sincerely hope that we have not omitted anyone who has contributed to this project.

Jean Bradley Anderson
Lewis Anderson
James Applewhite
Geoff Archer

Laura Liljequist Ayres
Eleanor Bates
Andrea Bedell
Dave Bell

Frederick Berry
David Bevington
Phil Bisesi
Julia Blackwood

William Boggess
Edwin Booth
Gail Boyarsky and
  Walter Fowler

Richard Broadwell
Norm Brocard
Keith Brodie
Chiru Chang
Norm Christensen
Jim Clark
Steve Cummer
Randy Daniel
Dennis Darnell
Steve Davis
Sandy Davison
Patrick Dougherty
Mark Dreyfors
Robert Durden
George Dutrow
Judson Edeburn
Jeane Eichinger
Rachel Frankel
John R. Frazier
Daniel Gelbert
Frank Gilliam

O. C. Goodwin
Mona Grizwold
Dolores Hall
Steve Hall
Becky Heron
Duncan Heron
Michelle Hersh
Mark Hollberg
Zakiya Holmes
Ted Howard
Barry Jacobs
Terry W. Johnson
Nan Keohane
John King
Peter Klopfer
Ken Knoerr
Jane Korest
Ryan Lafrenz
Peter Lange
Jim Lee
Joe Liles

Merrill Lynch
Tom Magnuson
Jack H. Markley
Jeff Masten
Delbert Mayse
Tim Mohin
Jason Mubarak
B. B. Olive
Albert Ottinger
Robert Peet
Jeff Pippen
Boyd Post
Dan Richter
Atlas Rigsbee
William Schlesinger
Paul Saunders
Richard Seale
Rich Shaw and
  Holly Reid
Bob Schultz
William H. Sites

Richard Smith
Bruce Sorrie
David Southern
William Stambaugh
Craig Stow
Bob Strayhorn
Lauren Stulgis
Terry Tait
Tom Terry
Tallman Trask
Andrea Tresse
Rytas Vilgalys
Trawick Ward
J. A. Watson Jr.
Fred White
Glenn Whitfield
Clayton Wray

Opening page photos

Chapter 1: Check dams and terraces installed to remedy gullying in badly eroding abandoned field. Durham Division, Duke Forest, 1933. Photo by C. F. Korstian. Duke Forest Photo Collection.

Chapter 2: View of campus construction, 1929. Duke University Archives.

Chapter 3: Evidence of past human activity, such as this rock wall, is present in many parts of the Duke Forest. Photo by Ida Phillips Lynch.

Chapter 4: Dr. Korstian instructs a group of students from West Virginia University, 1953. Duke Forest Photo Collection.

Chapter 5: Research sites often require structures to facilitate access to the forest canopy. Duke Forest Photo Collection.

Chapter 6: Sustainable harvesting of timber resources on the Duke Forest has been part of its management since 1931. Duke Forest Photo Collection.

Chapter 7: Hikers enjoy a crisp fall day in the Duke Forest. Photo by Richard Broadwell. Duke Forest Photo Collection.

Appendix: Entrance sign along N.C. 751. Duke Forest Photo Collection.

Foreword

Recollections of Field Work of a July Morning

Norman L. Christensen Jr.

I HAVE LEARNED THAT, come summertime in North Carolina, it is best to begin your labors early, before sweat glues you to your clothes and data sheets. Knowing that lesson is what brought me to permanent sample plots 41 and 42 at what most of my colleagues consider an ungodly hour.

Plots 41 and 42 are in a 20-or-so-acre pine forest and are of interest to me because every pine in that wood was within three years of being 90 years old, all having invaded an old field left fallow during Reconstruction. A rather thoughtful forester, who must have perceived that he would not outlive this experiment, had numbered and measured each tree on those plots when they could still be measured with the fingers of one hand, thumbs and fingers touching. Many of those numbers and their trees were now gone, and I, armed with the data of 50 years, intended to divine the rules by which the forest died—yet grew.

The furrows of that old field were still obvious, though covered with pine needles, and even now they paid little attention to the natural contours of the hillside. Initially preserved by vagrants—aster, goldenrod, broomsedge, and the like—their rows were eventually fossilized by the unseen parts of more permanent residents.

The old-field grasses had long ago been displaced by more shade-tolerant forbs such as wild ginger, rattlesnake plantain, and wintergreen. The presence of Solomon's seal, jack-in-the-pulpit, and lady slipper orchid confirmed in a manner more eloquent than any instrumentation I could devise that this was a very favorable site: a habitat with ample moisture on a soil probably derived from calcium-magnesium rich volcanic rocks. A mere 400 million years ago, the rock from which this soil weathered was a part of a volcanic structure in the majestic ancient Appalachians—now eroded to a piedmont. Between the pines overhead and the herbs underfoot were scattered saplings of sweetgum, oaks, and hickories . . . but not young pines, a sure sign that I too would not outlive this experiment.

I walked down this gentle north-facing slope, noticing as I went that I was treading on a mat of club moss, a direct descendant of plants that vegetated the ancient highlands of this region. Turning toward the east and half squinting as I passed through scattered ribbons of misty summer morning sun, the carpet abruptly changed. It had become a dew-covered sea of dark green foliage and lavender flowers, periwinkle by name, a true immigrant, now a naturalized citizen, traveling from Europe to America among other immigrants.

As I surveyed this peculiar acre or two, I saw three stone slabs—three limestone monuments at the apex of three oblong depressions in the soil and guarded by several obviously ancient red cedars. Despite over a century's weathering, the inscriptions were still bold:

John Robson ~ died 1842 ~ age 21
William Robson ~ died April 4, 1871 ~ age 71
Ann Robson ~ died February 7, 1872 ~ age 70

Other shallow depressions surrounding me left no doubt that I was in the midst of a number of Robsons.

For a moment I looked around and the forest was gone—save those red cedars, which now gave a sparse shade to this small family cemetery. The furrows were fresh—this Scottish-Methodist family had discovered the land of milk and honey: they had cleared the land, exposing the red clay solum that had been weathering there undisturbed for the previous 70 million years; using the best technology then available, those Robsons worked to make the ground produce what humans need, or think they need.

Not since North Africa had separated from North America, 200 million years before, had this hill seen such rapid change. Initially the land was productive. The family flourished and played a significant role in the establishment of a small settlement and mill 500 yards downslope along New Hope Creek. But each year, cropping and accelerated erosion removed more of those few nutrients with which these soils were originally endowed. By the time John died, probably of typhus, production was already declining and they were getting fewer bushels, bales, and bunches from each acre. Dry years were hitting harder and William was borrowing larger sums of money. By the start of the Civil War poor years far outnumbered good years. This farm never quite recovered from the war. One autumn day, a man and a woman walked out of that field wiping the ancient clay from their hands one last time.

Instantly, the pines were there again. My thoughts shifted to my unfinished work and the chiggers crawling up my legs. It has been more than 100 years since the passing of William and Ann Robson. They have occupied my thoughts often since I visited their farm. They came and went. All things come and go. I think there is more.

– From *Duke University Letters*,
no. 33, March 31, 1982

Norman L. Christensen Jr., is professor of ecology and founding dean of the Nicholas School of the Environment and Earth Sciences.

Chapter 1
Origins of the Duke Forest

"The primal Piedmont is gone utterly."
– Michael A. Godfrey, *Field Guide to the Piedmont*

Hᴏᴡ ʏᴏᴜ ᴠɪᴇᴡ Dᴜᴋᴇ Fᴏʀᴇsᴛ depends on your perspective. Walk through these peaceful woodlands with a few different people, and you will sense the many filters through which people view the Forest.

Researchers and students have spent countless hours in these piney woods, puzzling over questions that will impact people all around the planet. Historians admire the forest's archaeological sites and view the land as a microcosm of the Piedmont past.

Hikers are drawn to the 87-mile network of gravel roads and foot trails that crisscross the rich forests and border scenic New Hope Creek, traversing rock outcrops and passing alongside the creek's meanders and backwaters. A biologist might view the Forest as a landscape in succession or a landscape in recovery. Conservation philosopher Aldo Leopold rued the fact that "one of the penalties of an ecological education is that one lives alone in a world of wounds." And certainly the treadmarks of modern society—urbanization, fragmentation, and deforestation—have blemished, and in some cases destroyed, many of the historically wild places in North Carolina's Piedmont region.

Duke University does not manage Duke Forest as an untouchable nature preserve: the property is primarily used as an outdoor research and teaching laboratory, and sections of the 7,046-acre holding are actively managed to generate timber revenue for operating the facility. Research projects dot the landscape, and flagging, sensors, and towers and other research paraphernalia are scattered around the Forest's six divisions. Yet Duke Forest still contains vestiges of the Piedmont's past landcover that have vanished elsewhere. Despite thousands of years of human manipulation, the forest harbors pockets of natural resistance, where tangled vegetation is slowly overtaking the remnants of past human enterprise.

New Hope Creek, upstream from Erwin Road. Photo by Ida Phillips Lynch.

Piedmont Past

Sandwiched between the rugged front range of the Blue Ridge Mountains and the low-lying sprawling Coastal Plain, North Carolina's Piedmont region maintains a distinct identity, although it shares some of its neighboring provinces' features, particularly on the borderlands. The gently sloping Piedmont ranges in elevation from about 1,000 feet near its western border with the Blue Ridge escarpment, to 200 to 300 feet at the fall line, where the region slips into the sedimentary soil of the Coastal Plain. Numerous streams and rivers weave through the central Piedmont, including the Eno and Little Rivers and New Hope Creek. Duke Forest is located on the eastern side of the Piedmont and lies in part in the Carolina Slate Belt, which is underlain by metamorphic and igneous rock, and in part in the Durham Triassic Basin.

Triassic basins contain sedimentary rocks that are more easily eroded than the rocks of the Piedmont uplands. They are thought to be failed rift valleys that originated when the African continental plate pulled away from the North American plate.

Daniel D. Richter Jr., professor of soils and forest ecology at Duke University's Nicholas School of the Environment and Earth Sciences (NSEES), is fascinated by the geology of Duke Forest. "The Piedmont is one of the most ancient exposed landforms in the

New Hope Creek flows from the Carolina Slate Belt formation into the Triassic Basin. Photo by Ida Phillips Lynch.

Igneous sill in Triassic sandstone just south of the main entrance to West Campus on University Drive, 1933. Duke Forest Photo Collection.

Remnants of stone walls and house foundations are scattered throughout the Duke Forest. Duke Forest Photo Collection.

world," remarks Richter. "Duke Forest is special because all the Piedmont's major geological substrata are found here. Many of these geological features are found in the Durham Division along Highway 751—including the Durham Triassic Basin. Triassic basins occur sporadically like salt and pepper from the Bay of Fundy to the Connecticut River Valley and Virginia, and are scattered throughout the Carolinas. Some of the soils are richer in the Durham Basin, so this area appears to have been highly desired by early settlers."

For thousands of years North Carolina's landscape has experienced dramatic upheavals, first caused by natural causes and later through the unremitting toil of human hands. Glaciers did not extend as far south as present-day North Carolina during the last glacial period, which gripped the continent approximately 20,000 years ago, but the climate at that time was considerably cooler, and a boreal forest of spruce and jack pine dominated the region. When the glaciers receded some 10,000 years ago, the climate here grew milder, and deciduous species such as hickory and oak returned. As the climate continued to moderate, a new suite of species entered the forests, including chestnut, red maple, and sweetgum.

Archaeologists believe that humans first trickled into the Piedmont of North Carolina 12,000 to 13,000 years ago and may have overlapped for about 1,000 years with now-extinct megafauna. "During the full glacial period, mastodons, mammoth, horses, and bison may have roamed the area along with other now-extinct animals," writes archaeologist H. Trawick Ward in his book *Time before History*. "But evidence suggests that by the time the first people arrived, these animals were becoming extinct as a more modern vegetation pattern emerged."

The original Piedmont inhabitants modified the landscape in a number of ways. They built modest villages along major rivers and tributaries and burned open prairie-like areas in order to drive game. They traveled on old animal routes to trade with other tribes, creating trading paths that enabled them to access the resources of other regions, such as the invaluable rhyolite from the Uwharrie Mountains that was prized for creating spear points. Wielding arrows with shafts crafted from native shrubs such as arrowwood (*Viburnum dentatum*) they hunted deer, turkey, and small mammals. Today pot hunters still unearth their spear points, and their melodic tribal names still resonate in locations around the Triangle's urban jungle: Occaneechi, Eno, Shakori, and Haw.

Wild turkey (Meleagris gallopavo) *are now common on the Duke Forest. Photo by Jeffrey S. Pippen.*

Early Explorations

The arrival of European settlers in the Piedmont heralded sweeping changes for the wild landscape. John Lawson, the surveyor general for the Carolina colony, was likely one of the first Europeans to explore the land that eventually became Duke Forest. In 1701 he traveled through the hinterlands of North and South Carolina and wrote a travelogue of his adventures called *A New Voyage to Carolina*, which was published in 1709. As he journeyed through central North Carolina toward New Bern, he traveled through Hillsborough and eastward over the Eno River, and very likely passed through the present-day Hillsboro Division of Duke Forest. He visited Occaneechi Town on the Eno River, where he feasted on bear and venison with the Occaneechi tribe, and then continued southeastward on a "sad stony Way to Adshusheer," a route that may have led him in or near the Durham and Korstian

Divisions of the Forest to a Native American village on New Hope Creek. On his travels in the region he encountered "great Gangs of Turkies" and praised the beauty of the Piedmont, calling it the "Flower of Carolina."

Permanent European settlers were not far behind Lawson. The first settlers were primarily English and Scotch-Irish immigrants from Virginia and Pennsylvania who arrived in the Piedmont region in the 1740s. In *A Historical Sketch of New Hope Church*, published in 1886, Reverend D. I. Craig describes the settlers' new home with a touch of hyperbole: "About two hundred years ago the middle section of North Carolina was one wild and extensive wilderness, inhabited by savages and the wild beasts and birds of the forest." The Piedmont of yesterday was undoubtedly a much wilder place than today: virgin chestnuts and white oaks formed a dense forest cover and provided mast for a diversity of wildlife, including

"They found ample rivers and streams flowing through sometimes steep gorges and sometimes flat marsh and meadowland. But the overwhelming presence was the forest—endless, dark, filled with bird and beast and deep soil and huge timber. The aboriginal forest up to early historic times when the first settlers knew it provided a richer, more varied forest cover with far more edible fruits and nuts and more species of game animals than are found in the Piedmont today. Here were all the raw materials to sustain life and to provide the surplus for progress."

– Jean Bradley Anderson, *Durham County*

white-tailed deer, wild turkey, and the now-extinct passenger pigeon. Large mammals such as gray wolf likely prowled the woodlands. Waterways like New Hope Creek and the Eno River ran unchecked (except for beaver dams, which would have been a prominent feature in the landscape) and supported bountiful aquatic life: otter, mink, muskrats, and beaver, in addition to fish, mussels, and aquatic invertebrates.

The Europeans' efforts to tame the deep forests and shape the land to their needs quickly overshadowed any changes wrought by their Native American predecessors. Driven by the simple need to survive in an unfamiliar landscape, the early settlers adopted land-use practices that permanently altered the face of the Piedmont. These subsistence farmers grew and produced all of their food, tools, and clothing. In *The Duke Forest: A Demonstration and Research Laboratory*, Clarence Korstian, the first director of the Duke Forest, described the settlers' industriousness:

View from Piney Mountain looking southwest into the Triassic Basin. Duke Forest Photo Collection.

> The early settlers found a mild and healthful climate and fertile lands, but forest occupied vast areas, and their greatest task after they had built simple log cabins was to cut down the timber, clear the land, and prepare it for cultivation. The earlier settlers, locating on the fertile lands along the larger streams, grew corn, wheat, oats, rye, potatoes, and other vegetable. Indigo, hemp, and flax were important crops at an early date, but as the need for money grew, tobacco and cotton became important.

The settlers also systematically hunted the region's large mammals: Fearful of predators, they hunted gray wolves, black bears, and mountain lions until these were extirpated from North Carolina. They hunted wild turkey, white-tailed deer, and small mammals, greatly reducing their populations. Beavers were completely eliminated from the state before the turn of the 20th century. Smaller wildlife suffered as well: the Carolina parakeet, North America's only native parrot, may have nested in old-growth trees in bottomland habitats in the Piedmont, perhaps feeding on sycamores growing along New Hope Creek. This gregarious green and yellow bird was considered an orchard pest and was eventually hunted to extinction.

"The Piedmont is either plowed, paved, or in succession."

– Michael A. Godfrey, *Field Guide to the Piedmont*

The Piedmont in Succession

Early farming practices punished the Piedmont's highly erodable soils. Employing "slash and burn" techniques, farmers cleared forests to grow crops and abandoned the fields when the topsoil washed away and the land was no longer productive. In "An Ecological Analysis of the Plant Communities of Piedmont, North Carolina," published in *American Midland Naturalist* in July 1942, Duke University plant ecologist Henry J. Oosting explained how these farming practices altered the Piedmont landscape:

> In the early days of settlement, large tracts of forest were cleared for cultivation. Land was cheap and little thought was given to agricultural practices that would maintain soil productivity. The heavy winter rains soon washed away the best of the topsoil from unterraced fields and, after several years of cultivation without fertilizing, they became relatively unproductive. It became common practice to abandon such fields and clear new land.

These agricultural techniques exacerbated widespread soil erosion, along with the nature of precipitation in the Southeast. "Rainfall is very erosive to bare plowed soil in the South, more than two to five-fold more erosive than in New England," says Daniel Richter. "This is partly because the kinetic energy of rainfall hitting the soil increases as you move from the north to the south. And summer thunderstorms are much more intense and frequent in this region."

After the Civil War, the combination of short-sighted farming practices, the loss of soil fertility,

Old field in which erosion has reached the gully stage. Durham Division, Compartment 16. Duke Forest Photo Collection.

Durham Division, Compartment 51, looking east from N.C. Highway 751, about 1931. Photo by C. F. Korstian. Duke Forest Photo Collection.

and the allure of factory work in burgeoning cities such as Durham sparked a widespread abandonment of farms in the Piedmont that peaked in the 1920s and 1930s. The remaining "old fields" slowly began a transformation that created an unfamiliar landscape in Piedmont North Carolina. Derelict Piedmont farmland follows a fairly predictable pattern of regrowth called succession, a process through which habitats gradually regenerate following a disturbance such as clearing, storms, and fire. An area that is undergoing succession is colonized by an ever-changing kaleidoscope of plants that move in and flourish and then give way to other plants, in a generally organized fashion.

In the first year following field abandonment, broomstraw and other short-lived herbs colonize Piedmont old fields. In the next year or so, broomsedge,

"Palynologists have demonstrated that the vegetation of North America has been in a continuous state of flux for the past forty thousand years. Most ecologists agree that such variation has been the norm since the Pleistocene. It is now generally recognized that natural disturbance cycles, involving such agents as fire, wind, or pathogens, are a normal part of most landscapes and that few ecosystems ever achieve a steady-state climax. Furthermore, abundant data convince us that humankind has influenced the composition and structure of nearly all North American ecosystems for nearly ten thousand years."

– Norman L. Christensen Jr., "Landscape History and Ecological Change," *Journal of Forest History*, July 1989

Queen Anne's lace, and aster emerge. In about three years or so, pine seedlings appear and begin to overtake the herbaceous plants. In 30 to 70 years, the pine forest matures and young hardwood trees appear in the understory. Seventy-five to 100 years after the field is abandoned, hardwoods begin to replace the

View showing early succession in natural regeneration area, Durham Division, Compartment 66, 1939. Photo by W. R. Boggess. Duke Forest Photo Collection.

pines, until the old field is transformed into an oak-hickory forest on upland areas. A different tree community develops in moist lowland areas, often dominated by sweet gum and yellow poplar. Much of the early research on succession took place in Duke Forest and concepts that were established then are still applicable today.

Duke Forest through Korstian's Eyes

When Clarence F. Korstian assumed management of the Forest in 1931, the property comprised 4,696 acres, with a mix of pine forest, hardwood forest, mixed forest, and active and abandoned agricultural land. Korstian was a meticulous record-keeper and writer; his reports and photographs provide a vivid visual image of the makeup of the Forest at that time, when the property was divided into the Durham, New Hope Creek, and Hillsboro divisions. At one time, most of the area had been placed in cultivation, cleared for pastureland and homesites, or logged. Korstian reported that "many stands of second-growth timber 10 to 70 years old occur in the Duke Forest on land which was at one time under cultivation, as shown by the old corn and cotton rows which are still discernible."

Approximately 35 percent of the forest was covered in almost pure pine forest of "even-aged, young to middle-aged stands, most of which invaded fields that were abandoned during or subsequent to the Civil War," according to Korstian. Many of the hardwood and hardwood-pine forests contained trees of different ages, and he determined that the "uneven-aged hardwood and mixed pine-hardwood stands are probably the remnants of old growth or virgin stands which have been culled over from time to time for the choicest material, but which have not been clear cut." The only old-growth forest remaining in Duke Forest was found on steep slopes, rocky

Along N.C. Highway 751, early 1930s. Photo by C. F. Korstian. Duke Forest Photo Collection.

Tree planting on an abandoned field site. Durham Division, Compartment 51, about 1931. Photo by C. F. Korstian. Duke Forest Photo Collection.

Bald cypress (Taxodium disticum), *planted in 1937. Duke Forest Photo Collection.*

outcrops, and wet bottomlands, areas that would have been inaccessible to loggers who had to log trees with hand tools and use mules to drag (or "snake") the logs out of the forest.

Upon his arrival at Duke, Korstian plunged into reforesting the former agricultural areas that made up about one-quarter of the property. He and his staff planted plantations of loblolly and shortleaf pine, red cedar, yellow poplar, and smaller experimental plots of bald cypress and southern white cedar, neither of which occur naturally in the Piedmont. As well, he began converting old farm paths into a network of gravel woods roads that are still used today.

The Lay of the Land

A walk in today's Duke Forest takes you through a mosaic of land types. On a short hike, you might see pine plantations, rocky bluffs overlooking New Hope Creek, open meadowlike areas, and strange Rube-Goldberg-like contraptions dangling from pine trees. (Those would be the research projects.) The 7,046-acre Forest is divided into six mostly noncontiguous tracts in Orange, Durham, and Alamance Counties: the Durham, Korstian, Eno, Hillsboro, Blackwood, and Dailey Divisions. The Durham and Korstian Divisions are the largest and most heavily visited sections and are located roughly between Duke's West Campus and the town of Chapel Hill.

The Forest is an ideal outdoor classroom for studying Piedmont forests, as it contains a complete cross-section of the woodlands found in the upper Coastal Plain and lower Piedmont of the Southeast. Hardwoods, particularly oak-hickory forest with beech, tulip poplar, and red oak, dominate upland areas. Bottomland hardwoods cover the seasonally inundated floodplains of the numerous creeks and streams that run through the Forest, including the New Hope, Piney Mountain, and Mud Creeks. A variety of pine forests are interspersed with the hardwoods, including loblolly pine forests that have self-seeded in old fields, as well as planted and managed loblolly pine plantations. "Duke Forest has a good diversity of habitats, including pine oak heaths, rhododendron bluffs, and rich basic forests, and a lot of these habitats are pretty impressive," says Steve Hall, an invertebrate zoologist with the North Carolina Natural Heritage Program. The various habitats boast sizeable species lists: The Forest is home to more than 30 species of mammals, 180 breeding bird species, 24 amphibian species, and 30 species of reptiles.

Freshwater mussels are common in New Hope Creek. Duke Forest Photo Collection.

Fowler's toad (Bufo fowleri). Duke Forest Photo Collection.

The Forest provides a critical buffer for streams such as New Hope Creek, which winds through the Korstian Division. Because the Forest is not developed, this section of the stream is safe from the pollution and runoff that plagues other Triangle waterways. The forested corridor also offers a safe passage for mammals such as river otter and bobcat that typically travel through riparian areas. New Hope Creek overall is considered one of the best mussel habitats in the Upper Cape Fear River basin, and although the section in the Forest has not been surveyed for mussels to date, nine species of mussels, including three state-endangered species, have been found upstream of the Korstian Division.

The narrow footpaths that run along the lush slopes of New Hope Creek in the Korstian Division are a favorite destination for hikers. In spring and early summer, the trail winds through a green tunnel of vegetation, where river oats and sedges sway over the path. Clumps of wildflowers decorate the slopes, with dwarf-crested iris, several varieties of trillium, and hepatica among the standouts. Rough, thick grape vines dangle from tulip poplars and sycamores, and lush poison ivy taunts hikers with its noxious three-fingered touch.

During the peak of the breeding season in May, neotropical migratory songbirds that have traveled from the tropics to nest transform the woods into an aviary. Louisiana waterthrushes bob their tails as they search for invertebrates in the stream. Gaudy scarlet tanagers flit around the trees. Wood thrushes flute from the shadowy green woods. Eastern phoebes hunker in nests built in crevices in sandstone bluffs over the creek. Year-round residents such as barred owls and red-shouldered hawks skulk or screech from the green glade as their mood dictates.

Red-shouldered hawk (Buteo lineatus). *Photo by Jeffrey S. Pippen.*

The terrestrial view is equally interesting. Garter snakes sun in the paths while their aquatic counterparts, the water snakes, swim in the creek along with mud turtles. Cope's gray treefrogs buzz from their hidden perches, and American toads and leopard frogs hop in and out of view. You are likely to encounter members of an overly abundant white-tailed deer population, as well as beaver and possibly wild turkey. More elusive mammals such as gray fox, bobcat, and coyote (a recent arrival) are known forest residents as well.

Catesby's trillium (Trillium catesbaei). *Photo by Jeffrey S. Pippen.*

The American beaver (Castor canadensis) *was once extirpated from our area but now inhabits Piedmont streams. Duke Forest Photo Collection.*

Mink and otter signs have been found along the banks of New Hope Creek and Mud Creek, but seeing these wary water-lovers is a rare treat.

Our Natural Heritage

Despite centuries of natural change and human use, Duke Forest is one of the few large intact tracts of woodland remaining in the paved-over and booming Triangle region of North Carolina. According to the Triangle Land Conservancy, a nonprofit land trust working in central North Carolina, the amount of land lost to development in the Triangle region increased by 50 percent between 1987 and 1997. The North Carolina Department of Environment and Natural Resources estimates that North Carolina loses 277 acres of open space every day. Unfortunately, people often choose to build their homes in areas that typically sustain a diversity of wildlife, such as hilltops, stream corridors, and the interior of forests.

To put it simply, more pavement, parking lots, people, and buildings make life more challenging for plants and animals. Mammals and birds are losing the corridors that enable them to travel safely while searching for food, mates, and shelter. "Large tracts of undeveloped land are becoming pretty scarce in the Triangle region, so some species that require large tracts are disappearing," says Hall. "Raptors like hawks and owls require lots of room for hunting and neotropical migrants need big tracts to avoid nest predation by cowbirds. Animals like box turtles and snakes are threatened by habitat fragmentation, road mortality, and direct human removal or persecution. So good-quality habitat in big tracts like the Duke Forest is becoming vital for the preservation of some of our species. Just as one example, the uncommon four-toed salamander *Hemidactylim scutatum* is found in the Duke Forest. This amphibian needs good-quality forest pools and seeps and is usually found away from human disturbance. Clear-cutting bottomland forests, drying up of wetlands,

and the trampling of breeding habitat located too close to trails have all been implicated in the decline of this species."

Eastern box turtle (Terrapene caroline carolina). *Duke Forest Photo Collection.*

As well, exploding populations of white-tailed deer and non-native invasive plants are wreaking havoc on natural habitats in the Forest. Just 30-some years ago, white-tailed deer were rarely seen in the Forest, but today, the deer population has increased one-hundredfold in part because of the absence of historical predators such as the gray wolf. This "native invasive species" is devastating populations of some native plants, and the deer browse line, where deer have completely defoliated the vegetation, is visible in some parts of the forest.

Unchecked by the pests that control their populations in their native countries, introduced invasive plants are exploding in some parts of the Forest. "*Microstegium*, Japanese honeysuckle, and multiflora rose usurp territory from native plants and crowd and shade them out," says Bruce Sorrie, a botanist with the North Carolina Natural Heritage Program and coauthor of the *Inventory of Orange County Natural Areas.* "This is creating a net loss of native biodiversity." Many of the old homesites and cemeteries in Duke Forest are now blanketed in a dense mat of *Microstegium vimineum* (Japanese stilt grass), one of the most noxious invaders. Duke Forest resource manager Judson Edeburn believes that this species increased dramatically after Hurricane Fran ripped through the forest in 1996.

Although the Forest is not a pristine natural area and is not managed as a wildlife refuge, in effect it plays that role. "You might call this large forested area a *de facto* refuge, since a lot of the surrounding land is in farmland and suburbia," says Sorrie. Hall agrees:

Japanese stilt grass (Microstegium vimineum) *has become a significant exotic plant problem in the Duke Forest.*

"If we feel some obligation to preserve native species, for whatever reason, we need to preserve big tracts of natural habitat. Duke Forest provides enough space for many species. Although it's not large enough to support black bears, we know it still supports bobcats, as indicated by the presence of their tracks along New Hope Creek."

For more than a decade, biologists such as Hall and Sorrie have conducted periodic ecological surveys in sections of Duke Forest to seek out the property's most pristine natural places. The N.C. Natural Heritage Program considers Duke Forest to contain "some of the best examples of mature, second-growth forest communities remaining in the North Carolina Piedmont region," according to a 1986 Heritage Program report. As well, biologists recognize the Forest's immense value for long-term research, because it was the birthplace of fundamental theories about old-field plant succession in the Piedmont and houses long-term study plots that provide an unparalleled trove of information about Piedmont plant communities. A Heritage Program report concluded that certain areas of the Forest had "a long-term value bordering on priceless" and recommended that the most significant sites be placed under some type of long-term protection.

In the fall of 2004, Duke University agreed to enroll 1,220 acres of Duke Forest in the North Carolina Registry of Natural Heritage Areas, a voluntary agreement that states that the University intends to maintain the land for the perpetuation of natural processes, natural communities, and rare species populations. Almost every division of Duke Forest contains one or several key natural areas that are considered ecologically significant on a county, regional, statewide, or national level.

The Natural Heritage Program was delighted with this agreement. "Duke is one of the few universities that has made a verbal commitment to protecting its key natural areas," says Hall. "Duke's registry of the Forest's natural areas is great because it represents some commitment on the part of the University to protect natural areas as natural areas. Although it's not legally binding, it represents a commitment. And it could possibly stimulate other institutions to do the same thing, because it shows that some universities find value in these natural lands that they own and don't just view them as encumbrances or financial assets."

The Henry J. Oosting Natural Area was established by action of the Duke University Board of Trustees in 1959. Duke Forest Photo Collection.

Duke Forest's Divisions

A snapshot of the Forest's six divisions and the registered Natural Heritage Areas offers a glimpse of the property's great diversity.

Durham Division

The Forest's largest division, the 2,463-acre Durham Division, is located in Durham and Orange County and is bisected by N.C. Highway 751. Duke University acquired much of this section between 1925 and 1947.

The tract is used extensively for teaching exercises and contains numerous long-term study plots. Over the years some of the acreage has been converted to homesite development, campus expansion, the Duke University Golf Course and Faculty Club, and the right-of-way for U.S. 15-501 Bypass. Although portions of this division have been more intensively managed, it is still a critical wildlife corridor with mature hardwood and pine stands.

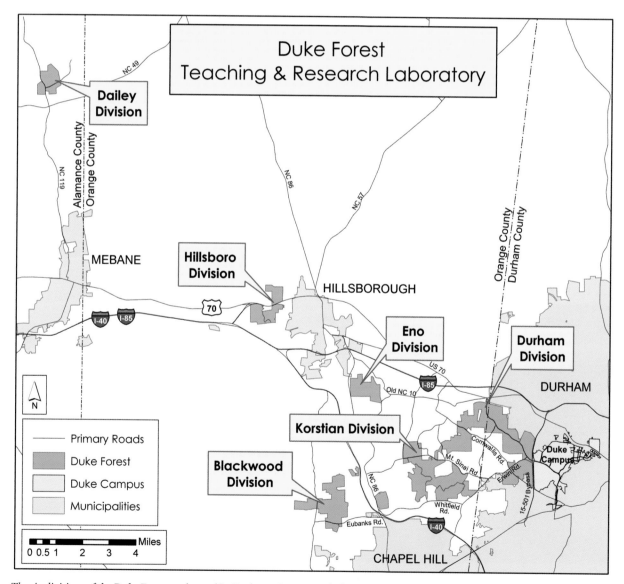

The six divisions of the Duke Forest are located in Durham, Orange, and Alamance Counties. Office of the Duke Forest.

Natural Heritage Areas

Gate 9 Pond: Several depressions in this low, swampy area are flooded part of the year and offer an ideal fish-free breeding site for 17 species of frogs, toads, and salamanders, including the rare four-toed salamander. In the springtime the area is alive with a cacophony of mating calls. Biologists from Duke and other universities have studied this area for many years.

Couch Mountain: Perched on the lip of the Triassic Basin, 640-foot Couch Mountain recalls the original forest encountered by early settlers in Orange County. The "mountain" is one of a northeast-oriented string of monadnocks found in Orange County, including Occoneechee, Bald, and Blackwood Mountains. These isolated hills are typically covered in a highly resistant rock layer that has not weathered as much as the surrounding landscape. A stately, old-growth white oak forest cloaks the summit of the mountain and contains some trees that are more than 300 years old and measure more than two feet in diameter. Deep-forest birds such as pileated woodpecker and hooded warbler inhabit the rich, old woods.

A Duke Forest road winds to the crest of Couch Mountain. Duke Forest Photo Collection.

Duke Forest Oak-Hickory Uplands: This mature forest is nearing old-growth quality and contains some trees measuring 30 inches in diameter. The area has been used as an intensive research site for more than 50 years.

Gate 4 Mafic Forests: These two tracts support several rare plant species: prairie dock, Earle's blazing star, and glade wild quinine.

Korstian Division

Located in the Chapel Hill Township of Orange County and originally called the New Hope Creek Division, the 1,777-acre C. F. Korstian Division ranks second to the Durham Division in terms of having the largest blocks of contiguous forest land. The University acquired the bulk of the division between 1925 and 1948. New Hope Creek winds through the center of the property, making it an important riverine corridor, which is widely recognized by conservation and local communities for its importance to the Triangle's water quality and open space network.

The Korstian Division is associated with two significant natural areas: the Henry J. Oosting Natural Area and the Johnston Mill Preserve. The Duke University Board of Trustees designated the 162-acre

Research on the four-toed salamander (Hemidactylium scutatum) *was conducted in the Duke Forest. Photo by Ida Phillips Lynch.*

Oosting parcel a Natural Area in 1959 and allows only "nonmanipulative" research in the property. The Triangle Land Conservancy's Johnston Mill Preserve, which contains an old-growth beech forest and the remnants of a gristmill dam, links the Oosting Natural Area to the Korstian Division along New Hope Creek.

Natural Heritage Areas

New Hope Creek Slopes: "This area is one of the most important study sites for both forestry and biology within the southeastern United States," according to the N.C. Natural Heritage Program. A five-mile section of New Hope Creek runs through the Korstian Division and is bordered by a rich riparian area with large mature trees such as sycamore and tulip poplar. The forests have a mountainous feel, with rocky outcrops and a lush spring wildflower display. The creek corridor offers great birding, as it has a wealth of breeding birds, including large raptors such as the barred owl and red-shouldered hawk, and neotropical migratory songbirds such as the scarlet tanager, Kentucky warbler, hooded warbler, and Louisiana waterthrush.

The cool microclimate of steep, north-facing bluffs along the waterway provide a refuge for such mountain species as mountain laurel, galax, and Catawba rhododendron. The Hollow Rock bluffs near Erwin Road are among the most memorable of these bluffs. Here the creek has carved a deep channel into the sandstone of the Triassic Basin, revealing a 20- to 30-foot-high sandstone bluff. Pockmarked and recessed sections of the bluff form dark grottoes over the creek and inspired the area's name. One of the more unusual creatures found on New Hope Creek's rocky bluffs is the bright red "sumo mite," which appears to be associated with north-facing slopes. "They're our biggest mite species and you can see them with your naked eye," says Hall. "They appear in the spring and the males form breeding congregations on tree trunks while the females wander up the trunks looking for a mate. The males

The New Hope Creek slopes. Duke Forest Photo Collection.

are very territorial, and when they encounter each other they wrestle and try to throw each other off the trunks." (Hence the name.)

Henry J. Oosting Natural Area: This natural area contains an impressive hardwood forest with large beech trees, but several hurricanes, including Fran in 1996, have battered the area and blown down many trees, creating wide swaths of downed timber. Old Field Creek, a tributary of New Hope Creek, runs through the natural area, and low-lying seeps provide good habitat for four-toed salamanders. In early spring, ephemeral wildflowers such as trout lily, windflower, and hepatica carpet the ground. A nine-year breeding bird census revealed that between 21 and 23 birds nest in the area, including the uncommon worm-eating warbler and broad-winged hawk. In 1959 the Executive Committee of the Duke University Board of Trustees approved the "establishment of a permanent natural area on Duke Forest lands for long range ecological research and related activity, the site selected to be agreed upon by the School of Forestry, the Department of Botany and the Department of Zoology." Named for an eminent Duke botanist, it was formally designated the Henry J. Oosting Natural Area in 1971.

Blackwood Division

The 1,120-acre Blackwood Division may deserve more superlatives than any other division of the Forest: it contains the only site in the Forest listed on the National Register of Historic Places; the highest point in the Forest, 751-foot Bald Mountain, is located within its boundaries; it is the site of the largest single research project ever conducted in the Forest, the FACE (Free-Air CO_2 Enrichment) project; and is the former battleground of one of the most heated (although bloodless) battles over local zoning, over the location of the Orange County Landfill.

Located in the Chapel Hill Township of Orange County, the division is made up of several parcels that were acquired primarily between 1944 and 1959. In 1991 the University acquired the 62-acre Neville tract west of Blackwood Mountain and connected two large sections of the division. The Triangle Land Conservancy's Pegg Hill Preserve borders the division on the west side of Old N.C. Highway 86. Recently Duke University acquired 61 additional acres to the east of Old N.C. Highway 86, and 16 acres along the road.

Natural Heritage Areas

Bald Mountain: The summit of this monadnock rises more than 200 feet above the surrounding terrain. One of Orange County's oldest chestnut oak forests cloaks the summit and offers a fertile habitat for a diversity of bird species such as pileated woodpecker, summer tanager, great-crested flycatcher, and hooded warbler.

Blackwood Mountain: This 744-foot monadnock is visible from Interstate 40 and Old N.C. Highway 86. The summit is covered in a mature oak-hickory and chestnut oak forest that is home to wild turkey and red-shouldered and red-tailed hawks.

Meadow Flats: This upland depression swamp forest grows on Orange County's most extensive area of Iredell soil. The soil drains very poorly, and standing water covers the area in the spring. Animals that typically inhabit bottomland habitats are found here, including American woodcock, red-shouldered hawk, Kentucky warbler, and the four-toed salamander.

Duke Forest Post Oak/Blackjack Oak Site: Orange County's only xeric hardpan forest, this site contains tree species such as post oak and blackjack oak that prefer dry conditions. Botanist Henry J. Oosting conducted much of his research in this area.

Chestnut oak (Quercus prinus) *and rocky outcrops cover the crest of Bald and Blackwood Mountains. Photo by Ida Phillips Lynch.*

Hillsboro Division

The Eno River flows in a southerly direction through the middle of the 587-acre Hillsboro Division, which is located in the Cheeks and Hillsborough Townships of Orange County. A five-acre quarry area, the source of the stone used in building Duke Chapel and many other campus buildings, is located in the southeastern section of the division. In 2000, Duke University sold a 63-acre tract on the north side of U.S. Highway 70 to Orange County; the tract is now protected as McGowan Creek Preserve.

Natural Heritage Area
Duke Forest Mesic Slopes: A two-mile stretch of forest along the Eno River upstream from Hillsborough provides important habitat for river otters, Carolina darters (fish), and notched rainbows (mussels). The presence of these species indicates the area's high water quality. Birds such as red-shouldered hawk and Kentucky warbler nest in the woodlands.

Eno Division

This 487-acre parcel was acquired between 1942 and 1957. The division is located in the Eno and Chapel Hill Townships of Orange County and contains several long-term research sites. The eastern edge of this division was once part of Benjamin Duke's 2,407-acre "gentleman's farm."

Natural Heritage Area
Stony Creek Spring: This flat, low-lying, boggy seep is covered in thick mats of sphagnum moss that provide perfect nesting habitat for the four-toed salamander. This state-listed Special Concern amphibian lays its eggs only under clumps of moss near springs and pools. Mud salamanders and red salamanders also prefer spring habitats and are probably found here. As well, the gray petaltail, a rare spring-inhabiting dragonfly, has been seen here.

Dailey Division

This 422-acre tract was acquired in 1965 and is located in the Pleasant Grove Township of Alamance County, north of the town of Mebane. The division contains managed pine plantations that have been used for several long-term research projects. Although the tract is somewhat remote from the University, the rural setting is ideal for certain forest management activities required by some research projects.

Rocky outcrops in Meadow Flats, one of the Natural Heritage Areas in the Duke Forest. Photo by Ida Phillips Lynch.

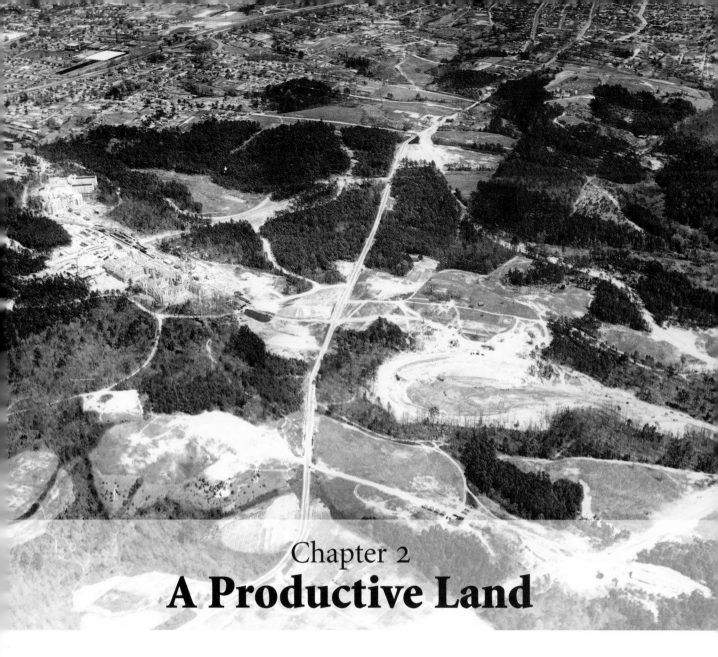

Chapter 2
A Productive Land

"IN THE SPRING OF 1924 Mr. Duke authorized us to begin the purchase of land adjacent to the campus of Trinity College. He had in mind the purchase of a good deal of land; for, as I once heard him say, he never knew when to stop buying land. We proceeded at once to get options and to buy, first land that adjoined the College, and then on into contiguous territory. The land was not especially desirable and was not easy to get. It came more and more to look as if we had a difficult task before us.

"In the meantime, one afternoon I took a walk with three of my sons out into the woods west of the College, and that afternoon I accidentally rediscovered a beautiful woodland tract to the west of the campus through which I had often passed in other years when I was given to horseback riding. It was for me a thrilling moment when I stood on a hill, looked out over this wooded tract, and realized that here at last is the land we have been looking for."

– William Preston Few, former president
of Duke University, "The Beginnings of an
American University," an unpublished manuscript.

William Preston Few, president of Trinity College 1910-1924, president of Duke University 1924-1940. Duke University Archives.

A casual walk in the woods inspired the direction of a land purchase that has borne unforeseen benefits for Duke University and the educational and research community as a whole. Since 1931, when the university acquired roughly 5,000 acres of woodlands and abandoned farmland in Durham and Orange Counties that formed the core of Duke Forest, the Forest has become one of the leading outdoor research and educational facilities in the United States. It is the site of hundreds of groundbreaking research projects and is a beloved outdoor classroom for students and faculty from Duke and other institutions. Ironically, the Forest's early champions approached its acquisition with strictly strategic business-oriented motives.

In *The Launching of Duke University*, a history of the formation of Duke University, Duke history professor emeritus Robert F. Durden described the University's purchase of Duke Forest as a "serendipitous acquisition of assets." Durden, who also wrote *The Dukes of Durham*, the definitive biography of the Duke family that built a global tobacco empire from a handful of bright leaf tobacco, devotes a chapter in *The Launching of Duke University* to a thorough exploration of how James B. Duke and William Few, president of Trinity College and later president of Duke University, directed the surreptitious purchase of 5,000 acres of worn-out farmland that became the future core of Duke Forest.

From 1921 until James B. Duke's death in 1925, Few and Duke led the campaign to transform Trinity College into a nationally recognized university. Duke provided both his financial backing and business acumen to creating a blueprint for the new institution that ultimately bore his name. Their plans called for expanding the existing college and building new medical, law, and engineering schools, among others. As the 108-acre Trinity campus in the town of Durham could not support these ambitious

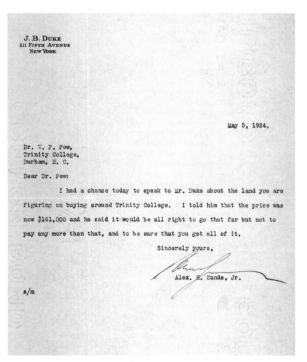

Letter regarding purchase of land. From A. H. Sands, secretary to B. N. Duke, to William Preston Few. Duke University Archives.

The entrance to Trinity College off Main Street, Durham. Duke University Archives.

expansion and construction plans, Duke and Few engineered a discreet campaign to purchase additional property for the University.

They initially intended to purchase land directly around the existing Trinity campus, but rumors that James B. Duke was bankrolling land purchases in the area spurred landowners to increase their prices. Duke became so frustrated by the sudden inflation that he threatened to relocate the university to Charlotte, but Few found the solution when he rediscovered his old haunts west of campus.

With James B. Duke's blessing and financial support, Robert Flowers, vice president of Trinity, enlisted local realtor Murray Jones to buy the land on behalf of the institution. "Flowers wanted to purchase this land in a secret fashion because they didn't want land prices to skyrocket, so they camouflaged the purchase by using an agent," Durden explained in a 2006 interview. Many of the landowners in the area had abandoned their worn-out farmland and were

Open land along Club Boulevard, 1938. Duke Forest Photo Collection.

struggling financially, making them willing sellers. Jones put the first parcel under option on November 7, 1924, and purchased close to 5,000 acres by 1929, mostly in small tracts from family holdings such as the Rigsbee and Pickett farms.

James B. Duke did not want these large tracts of land just for school buildings or campuses. Land acquisition was for him a sound business proposition, an opportunity to secure the success of the University as well as his commercial interests. In *The Launching of Duke University*, Durden notes that the Forest and the future School of Forestry:

> largely owed their existence to the unanticipated consequences of a shrewd industrialist-philanthropist's insistence on an access road, and, to a lesser extent, his interest in a potential water-power site. . . . The critical importance of having ample land was one of the basic lessons that J. B. Duke had learned over a lifetime of building large industrial enterprises. Another learned lesson, moreover, was that good access, in the form of roads or railways, was equally vital.

To ensure that larger population centers in the state had easy access to the University, Duke wanted to build a road to the campus that would link the Greensboro-Durham Highway (present-day N.C. Highway 70) to the Chapel Hill-Durham highway (present-day U.S. 15-501). "In order to get the land for the road, Flowers had to buy more than the highway right of way, so the land on either side of what became N.C. 751 became the core of Duke Forest," says Durden. "I don't think the purchase was just expansion, it was an accidental byproduct of the need for that road." Today Highway 751 runs right through the Durham Division in Duke Forest.

Duke's instincts for business also informed the purchase of the scenic sloping woodlands along New Hope Creek in the Forest's Korstian Division. "Duke had heard about a potential power site on New Hope Creek, so he asked that that land be purchased

N.C. Highway 751 at newly constructed Gate 7 in the 1930s. Duke Forest Photo Collection.

as well," explains Durden. "By that time Duke had been involved in the hydropower industry for 20 years or more and had purchased power sites throughout the Piedmont Carolinas, so I imagine that he purchased the New Hope Creek property as a possibility or a potentiality, but of course he didn't live long enough to see that happen." James B. Duke undoubtedly learned of the potential hydropower

James B. Duke, B. N. Duke, F. L Fuller, W. A Erwin, and J. S. Cobb crossing the bridge of the Cape Fear River, November 1902, near the town of Duke, North Carolina. In James B. Duke Papers, Rare Book, Manuscript, and Special Collections Library, Duke University, Durham, North Carolina.

site through his connection to the Erwin Cotton Mill Company: his older brother Ben was president of the textile mill. The company was founded in West Durham and owned much of the land along the portion of New Hope Creek upstream of Erwin Road.

In the letters exchanged by members of the Duke family, Few, and Flowers during 1924 and 1925, one can track the schemes and strategies behind the ongoing land purchases. Flowers wrote Benjamin Duke, on May 8, 1925, marveling at the result of the feverish land-buying spree:

> I wish I could take you out on the plateau on the Rigsbee Road. It is really a thing of beauty. The acquisition of the land has been to me one of the most absorbing things I have ever been connected with. There have been a great many difficulties but practically all of them have been over-come. The more I think about it the more I am convinced that the whole thing has been providential. To be able to acquire as much land as we have and connect it up with the present campus seems almost unbelievable.

In a letter to Mrs. James B. Duke dated September 8, 1925, Robert Flowers alluded to Duke's business interest in the land: "Mr. Duke is interested in water-rights below Patterson's mill, and where Sand Creek and Mud Creek enter New Hope River." The area around this parcel of land is, in fact, one of the most captivating sections of New Hope Creek, where the weighty stones of the remnant mill dam span the creek downstream from the sandstone Hollow Rock bluffs.

James B. Duke died in the midst of the land acquisition campaign, on October 25, 1925. But his death did not halt the expansion of the properties that came to form the Duke Forest. By 1929 the University had purchased approximately 5,000 acres at a cost of $1,762,617, according to Durden. This flurry of land purchases eventually spawned the establishment of a teaching

In addition to the Patterson and Robson mill sites, there are the remains of at least one more mill located on New Hope Creek in what is now the Duke Forest. Photo by Ida Phillips Lynch.

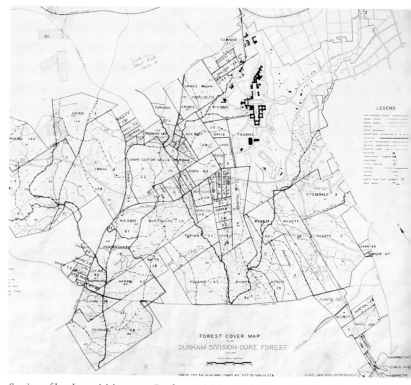

Section of land acquisition map, Durham Division, Duke Forest. Office of the Duke Forest.

and research forest and the Duke University School of Forestry. The eroded, exhausted farm fields thus gradually returned to productiveness, not by means of agriculture and the cultivation of traditional farm crops, but by the regeneration of a forest and the birth of the first graduate forestry program in the South.

Duke Stone

James B. Duke was engaged in many aspects of the construction of the new university and took a particular interest in design and construction of the new campus buildings. According to Durden, Few and his close associate Frank C. Brown, a professor of English, visited a number of northern colleges and universities in the spring of 1924, gathering ideas and blueprints for the university's buildings and landscaping. Clearly impressed with the buildings at Princeton, Bryn Mawr, and Yale, Duke and his architect, Horace Trumbauer, consulted with Few and decided that the new buildings should be constructed in stone in the Tudor Gothic style.

Initially, the construction team began ordering samples of stone from established quarries in northern states such as Pennsylvania, New Jersey, and Massachusetts. "Frank C. Brown, in the meantime, checked out the possibility of North Carolina stone and found in the possession of the state geologist some specimens of volcanic stone from an abandoned quarry near Hillsborough," writes Durden in *The Dukes of Durham*. Duke and the university staff were delighted with the mosaic of colors in the stone, which has seventeen different shades of blue, yellow, green, gray, black, and brown. He was also pleased by the cost savings: the Hillsborough stone cost $3.55 per ton compared with upward of $15.00 a ton for the Princeton stone.

In typical James B. Duke style, he requested the purchase of the entire quarry, which now comprises a five-acre section of the Hillsboro Division of the

Duke Quarry, 1927, in what would later become the Hillsboro Division of the Duke Forest. Duke University Archives.

Duke Quarry, 1928. Duke University Archives.

Forest. The quarry provided the stone for many of the landmark buildings on campus, including Duke Chapel and Cameron Indoor Stadium. The quarry stone, which occurs in the Carolina Slate Belt, is a metamorphic rock called phyllite and is relatively easy to split. "Duke Stone" is still used in construction on the Duke campus, such as in the West-Edens Link, the Wilson Recreation Center, and an addition to the Duke Divinity School. Today, the stone costs approximately $120 per ton.

Quarried stone ready for delivery to construction on campus, 2003. Duke Forest Photo Collection.

Rail cars loaded at the Duke Quarry were taken directly to the new campus under construction, 1929. Duke University Archives.

Chapter 3
The Place and Its People

"FOR MORE THAN TWO HUNDRED YEARS a wave of agriculture rolled across our landscape. The deep woods were turned to cropland and pasture. But the tide turned . . . and agricultural life has been, for the most part, retreating from the land. Left undisturbed, forest reclaims open land quietly and completely. It is ironic that what former generations wanted out of the way in their time is today an enduring visual proof of their existence: collections of stone."

– Dan Snow, *In the Company of Stone: The Art of the Stone Wall*

Cryptic rock formations are scattered throughout Duke Forest. Walking down the western slope of Piney Mountain in the Forest's Korstian Division, David Southern and I come across a circular mound of rocks about two feet tall that seems to have been arranged with some semblance of order. We spot five other rock mounds solidly entrenched in the earth, tree shadows playing around them. Southern is an editor at Duke University Press and a historian who has boundless enthusiasm and curiosity for history on both the local and global scale. He lived about a mile from the Hollow Rock Store on Erwin Road for 32 years, and Duke Forest is his old territory. As we walk through the woods on this overcast April day, he shares tidbits of local lore and history that I hurriedly scribble down in my notebook.

Standing beneath the pale green spring canopy, we talk about the origin of these rock piles, musing about whether they could be Native American cairns, or whether farmers used them to control erosion, or whether they were simply tossed aside as settlers cleared the woodland for plowing. "Stones were heartbreaking things," says Southern. "They can hobble horses and break plows, so farmers removed them from fields when they could." Although the Native American theory seems more romantic, we eventually decide that it is unlikely, and continue walking through the dim woods toward New Hope Creek.

The traces of Duke Forest's past inhabitants are inscribed in stone: spear points, building foundations, chimneys, rock walls, and grave markers. Some of these cultural records have clear origins, such as the remnants of the Patterson and Robson gristmills on New Hope Creek. But the more you dig into the past here, the more questions arise. Since only a few archaeological surveys have been conducted in the Forest's six disjunct divisions, sometimes you just have to speculate. Who built the rock wall beneath the old white oak in the Eno Division? What was historian William Boyd referring to when he wrote that "Indians undoubtedly had a village of considerable size at Patterson's Mill" in *The Story of Durham*?

Low rock walls, crumbling house foundations, unmarked gravestones, fence posts, deep erosion

Most old tobacco barns such as this one on the Duke Forest have collapsed and their foundations are all that remain. Duke Forest Photo Collection.

Remains of Robson's Mill, Korstian Division. Photo by Ida Phillips Lynch.

gullies, faint road beds, and a few mill dams are tantalizing traces of Duke Forest's past. Historians know enough about these remnants to piece together the human history in select areas of the Forest. Their work tells us that the Forest's past land use mirrors that of the Piedmont overall.

One of several family grave sites in the Duke Forest. Duke Forest Photo Collection.

Natural springs once provided drinking water for many home sites. Duke Forest Photo Collection.

"A new degree in scholarship is taken as soon as we learn to read in the woods as well as we read in the study."

– Ralph Waldo Emerson, *Nature*, 1838

Reading the Landscape

Clues imbedded in the landscape can provide a biography of past residents and their impacts on the land. In "Landscape History and Ecological Change," published in the July 1989 *Journal of Forest History*, Norman L. Christensen Jr., professor of ecology and founding dean of the Nicholas School of the Environment and Earth Sciences, explains how the plant world can provide a record of past human activity:

> The species that compose a forest community can also provide information about its past. The presence of shade-intolerant trees in the forest canopy is usually a sign of past disturbance. This is true today in the southeastern United States, where shade-intolerant trees such as pine or tulip tree in the forest canopy provide a reliable measure of the nature and extent of past disturbance. . . . Even some herbaceous plants indicate past forest history. For example, in forests of the southeastern U.S. piedmont, the common garden periwinkle (*Vinca minor*) is a faithful indicator of the location of old homesites and graveyards.

Learning to interpret these vestiges of the past takes time. "As they walk around the Duke Campus, some students see the big trees and feel like they're walking through an ancient forest," says Christensen. "But 130 years ago, Duke's campus was a cotton field. If you look very closely you can see the gullies and rows where cotton was planted. There have been enormous changes in this area, and people are often astounded to learn what happened here in the past."

Christensen has used Duke Forest as his outdoor classroom for 30 years, and the Forest is prominently featured in some of his classes. On a muggy August day in 2005, Christensen led one such class, a group of incoming Nicholas School students, on a walk to one of his favorite spots in the Forest: the Wooden Bridge on New Hope Creek.

"To understand this forest you have to understand people's interactions as well," he told the attentive group. He then summarized the changes reflected in the evolving woodlands of Duke Forest. He described the collisions between Native American and European culture, the shift from subsistence farming to market farming in the Piedmont, and the "social downward spiral that was tied to the decline of the landscape." He told the students that they were standing just downstream from the ruins of the

Robson gristmill and homeplace, where a family's fortunes were intimately tied to their environment. This family of Scotch-English settlers dammed the creek and built a stone and wooden gristmill that served the local community and may have sparked the growth of other cottage industries. But by 1880 the mill pond had backed up with sediment, and New Hope Creek's mill culture was in decline.

Seeing how humans and nature have shaped this small section of the forest underscores Duke Forest's great value as a place to observe the effects of land use and settlement. "The Forest is a continuum that goes all the way back to when it was forest primeval," explains Christensen. "You can look at the Forest and imagine its deep history, as well as its future."

The bridge over New Hope Creek between Compartments 16 and 19, New Hope Creek Division, built by the Civilian Conservation Corps with material provided by Duke Forest staff, 1934. Duke Forest Photo Collection.

Native Americans in the Duke Forest

As David Southern and I wend our way toward Piney Mountain, we stop to admire a clump of crested dwarf iris blooming atop a boulder on the bank of New Hope Creek. We carefully cross a log over Piney Mountain Creek, and I see a mud turtle swimming in the water. Sedum with white flowers covers a rocky outcrop at the base of Piney Mountain, where wizened cedar trees grow in the sparse soil.

Standing on the outcrop, Southern spots what he was looking for: a line of rocks extending across part of New Hope Creek that forms an eddy in the current. Years ago while researching in deed books, he came across an old estate division that referred to a "fish dam" on this section of the creek. Intrigued, he hiked here and constructed a basket from muscadine and honeysuckle vines in the Native American tradition, and waded

The dwarf crested iris (Iris cristata) is one of the many showy spring flowers in the Duke Forest. Photo by Jeffrey S. Pippen.

into the water behind the line of rocks and caught a little fish. "It's just a natural, accidental string of rocks that forms a barrier in the creek, and with a bit of human manipulation, it became an effective fish trap," he says with a bemused look on his face.

Archaeology in North Carolina's Piedmont region is a relatively young field. Many of the region's archaeological surveys were initiated in order to excavate and catalog artifacts from sites slated to be flooded by the construction of reservoirs, such as Falls and Jordan Lakes. Although most of the archaeological research conducted in Duke Forest has focused on early European settlements, there are some clues about the first inhabitants.

People first appeared in North Carolina's Piedmont approximately 12,000 to 13,000 years ago, but little evidence of these Paleo-Indians remains except for the fluted spear points that turn up occasionally in plowed fields and river floodplains. Archaeologists conjecture that Paleo-Indians of the Piedmont survived by hunting small mammals and foraging for nuts, seeds, and fruits, but the lack of solid evidence of their passage led archaeologist Trawick Ward, author of *Time before History*, to dub the Paleo-Indian period in North Carolina a "hazy world." The archaeological record provides more information about the Archaic period, the next phase of Native

New Hope Creek in the Korstian Division. Photo by Jeffrey S. Pippen.

American culture, which lasted from about 8000 to 1000 B.C. Archaeologist Randy Daniel, a professor at East Carolina University, has some hypotheses about Native American activity around present-day Duke Forest during that time period. In 1993, Daniel surveyed the Korstian and Blackwood divisions of the Forest while conducting a comprehensive archaeological study for Orange County. Most of his findings in the county dated from the middle to late Archaic period, approximately 6000 to 1000 B.C.

"Archaic folk were hunters and gatherers," explains Daniel. "Agriculture did not develop until about A.D. 1000, so in the Archaic period Native Americans spent most of their time hunting game and gathering wild food sources. Because of their diet, they could not live permanently in one place, because they would literally eat themselves out of house and home. So it was in their nature to be somewhat nomadic and follow the resources seasonally."

If Native American tribes roamed through present-day Duke Forest, they probably set up temporary hunting camps along ridges and knolls overlooking the rich bottomlands along New Hope, Sand, and Mud Creeks. In addition to white-tailed deer, they hunted wild turkey and mammals such as black bear, rabbit, opossum, gray squirrel, and raccoon. They burned areas of woodland to drive game in "fire drives." They also caught turtles and fished, possibly by building weirs in the creeks. Archaeologists have found concentrations of rock shards on hillsides in the Forest that are thought to have been quarry sites where Native Americans gathered stones to craft spear points and other tools.

Native American culture changed dramatically during the Woodland period, which extended from approximately 1000 B.C. to about A.D. 1600. "Three interrelated innovations marked the end of the Archaic period and the beginning of the Woodland period: pottery-making, semisedentary villages, and horticulture," writes Ward in *Time before History*. A few woodland sites have been excavated in Orange County, along the Eno River near Occaneechi Town,

but evidence found to date leads Daniel to believe that "other than the Eno River villages, Woodland occupation in Orange County was probably limited to hunting trips or other special forays."

The clearest traces of Native American culture after A.D. 1000 in the central Piedmont have been excavated from settlements in the bottomlands of the Eno, Flat, and Haw Rivers and their tributaries. In the early 1700s, small Siouan-speaking tribes inhabited Orange and Chatham Counties, including the Eno, Occaneechi, Adshusheer, Shocoree, and Sissipihaw. Their culture and lifestyle were notably similar: "All built villages of circular bark houses along the rivers and creeks," writes archaeologist James H. Merrell in *Excavating Occaneechi Town*. "All followed a seasonal subsistence routine that balanced farming the bottomlands along the river, fishing the nearby waterways, hunting in the hills or canebrakes, and gathering wild plants at selected sites." Perhaps the Occaneechi Indians, who settled near Hillsborough, traveled through the Duke Forest woodlands in search of prey.

When the first European settlers arrived in Piedmont North Carolina in the 1740s, they found a landscape that had been modified by Native Americans. "Animals seeking salt licks, water holes, and fording places, and Indians following their prey or traversing their blazed paths on the ridges had threaded the forest with trails which the explorers and traders made use of," writes historian and genealogist Jean Bradley Anderson in her book *Durham County*.

> Primary among the trails was an ancient route known to the Europeans as the Indian Trading Path or the Occaneechi Trail. It led from present Augusta, Georgia, to the Catawba Indians near the North Carolina border, northeast across North Carolina (passing through what would become Durham County) to Fort Henry, an important trading post in Virginia now known as Petersburg, on up to Bermuda Hundred on the James River.

The Trading Path provided the Native American tribes with an important trade route for exchanging spear points, baskets, and pottery with distant tribes and for trading deerskins for European goods such as knives, toys, and later, guns and alcohol. The exact route of the Trading Path is hotly debated among local historians, but it is thought to have roughly paralleled today's Interstate 85, running near present-day Duke Forest. The trail crossed the Eno River west of Hillsborough and may have extended into the Forest in the Hillsboro Division.

John Lawson, the young surveyor general of the Carolina colony, traveled on the Trading Path as he explored the hinterlands of North and South Carolina. He witnessed the waning of Native American culture in the Piedmont: when he visited Occaneechi Town in 1701, the original inhabitants were suffering from the effects of ills that arrived in the country with the Europeans, including a medley of diseases such as smallpox and measles. By the time the first land grants were issued in Piedmont North Carolina, Native Americans had almost faded from the region and many of them had retreated to other states to join the remnants of other tribes, such as the Catawba Indians in South Carolina. "Except for a few scattered, isolated families whose relatives remain in the region today, the first Europeans to permanently settle in the North Carolina Piedmont found only abandoned villages and vacant fields," writes Ward.

European Settlers

When Europeans began trickling into present-day Durham and Orange Counties in the 1740s, the untrammeled Piedmont was called the "backcountry" or "Hill-Country." Most of these early settlers journeyed from northern states and North Carolina's coast in search of cheap, fertile farm land. A wave of English settlers emigrated from the first North Carolina settlements in the eastern part of the state, and another group traveled from Virginia on the Indian Trading Path. A tremendous influx of German and Scotch-Irish settlers entered the region by following the Great Philadelphia Wagon Road from Pennsylvania, New Jersey, and Maryland.

These Europeans settled in the area that eventually became Orange County, a region that early North Carolina historian Francis Nash described in biblical terms in 1910: "In its genesis, Orange County, like the earth, was without form and void."

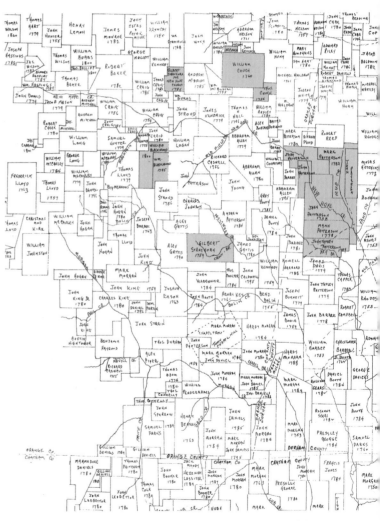

This map, prepared in 1973 by A. B. Markham, depicts a portion of the original "old Orange County" land grants and shows parts of the present Orange, Chatham, and Durham Counties. The names Strayhorn, Blackwood, Couch, and Patterson are discernible, among many others. Courtesy of Annie P. Markham and A. B. Markham, Jr.

In fact, when the county was formed in 1752, it had distinct boundaries and comprised some 3,500 square miles, extending from Virginia southward to the northern portion of present-day Lee County. Between 1770 and 1881, Orange was whittled down as portions of the region were carved out to create 10 new counties, including Durham, where part of Duke Forest now lies.

"It was a country of high hills and narrow valleys, with here and there gray, gravelly ridges, or elevated plateaus with much intermixture of sand with clay. The valleys were always fertile. The hillsides and tops and sandy uplands were only moderately so, while the gravelly ridges were generally poor and non-productive. Throughout all this territory, except on the poorer ridges, the forest growth was magnificent, with the oaks predominating. The soil seemed peculiarly adapted to the flourishing growth of all the hard wood, deciduous trees. Oaks four feet in diameter at their base were not uncommon, and occasional specimens six feet in diameter were found. Along the streams these oaks and hickories, birches, beeches, poplars and sycamores towered high, and the elm and the maple attained unusual size and unusual magnificence of foliage. There are remains of these forests to-day, which testify to their pristine grandeur."

– Francis Nash, "The History of Orange County,"
The North Carolina Booklet, October 1910

Whether they were fleeing religious persecution and economic hardship in their native Europe, or escaping the already crowded northern colonies, the settlers must have been pleased with this hospitable, sparsely settled region, which Nash proclaimed "one of the most beautiful sections of North Carolina." The rich floodplains of the Haw, Eno, Little, and Flat Rivers, and tributaries such as New Hope Creek in the southern part of the county provided farm and pasture land. The homesteaders coveted land on or near a water source, so many of the early land grants

spanned out from waterways. Once settlers located a desirable tract of land they went through the cumbersome process of obtaining a land grant from Lord Granville, one of the original Lords Proprietors, who held title to 26,000 square miles of North Carolina. Most of the early land grants were between 100 and 500 acres. Although the first settlers did not leave extensive written records, researchers and genealogists have compiled histories of some of the first colonists to settle in present-day Duke Forest and neighboring areas.

Finding New Hope

In a shady, low-lying grove of red cedars off of N.C. Highway 86, a few miles from Duke Forest's Eno Division, you can visit the graves of some of the first Europeans who settled in and around the Forest's Eno, Korstian, and Blackwood Divisions. More than 200 hand-incised and unmarked gravestones mark the resting places of the founders of the New Hope Church. In early spring, blooming ephemerals such as blue-eyed grass, green-and-gold, and periwinkle add color to the grays and browns of the stones and cedars. A mottled gray stone marks the site of the original New Hope Presbyterian Church, which was built here about 1756. The founders of the church, who may have migrated from the same area in northern Ireland, had originally settled along the Haw River in an area called Hawfields in the late 1740s, where they founded Hawfields Church in 1755. Hearing rumors that their land grants might be disputed, several of the families, including William Craige and Gilbert Strayhorn, moved 10 miles eastward to claim land along New Hope Creek, where they founded New Hope Presbyterian Church.

New Hope Presbyterian Church Cemetery. Photo by Ida Phillips Lynch.

Springing from its source in western Orange County near Hillsborough, New Hope Creek flows southeastward into Durham and Chatham Counties and drains into the Cape Fear River (what is today the Jordan Reservoir). In *A Historical Sketch of New Hope Church in Orange County, N.C.*, Reverend David I. Craig noted that "for more than a century it [New Hope Creek] was famous for its abundant production of fish, and at the present time few streams of like size yield a better supply or quality." Craig describes how the pilgrims named their new home:

> They came into the neighborhood of New Hope, where they saw rich bottoms, numerous creeks and springs, spacious meadow lands, and fine forest trees. They had an eye for the best lands, and here—after weary wanderings, untold hardships, and anxieties of body and mind—they were inspired with "new hopes," and at once determined upon their permanent home. They looked upon the prospect and called it a "New Hope." This is the explanation that has been handed down to me through generations, of the origin of the name of the stream which is called "New Hope" unto this day.

The founding families spanned out around the nearby landscape and established homesteads along the creek and nearby waterways such as the Eno River. William Craige (the family name later became Craig) "settled, lived and died about two or three miles west of the church, on the south bank of New Hope stream." He and his four sons owned "all the lands on both sides of New Hope stream, several miles in width and extending up and down the stream, . . . to the present possessions of William Robson, on the road leading from Hillsboro to Chapel Hill, embracing a large area of country south and west from the church," according to David Craig. William Robson operated a gristmill on New Hope Creek in the 1800s. Gilbert Strayhorn settled along present-day New Hope Church Road, near Duke Forest's Eno Division, and later amassed a large property that bordered the Craig holdings on New Hope Creek.

Farther afield, "William Blackwood, one of the first settlers, and also the Kirkland family, located to the south-west of the Craigs, and owned large bodies of land known to this day as 'the big meadows,'" writes Craig in his *Historical Sketch of New Hope Church*. "And to the east of these lands is quite an elevation, which has always been known as 'the Blackwood mountain.'" Today, 744-foot Blackwood Mountain is a prominent feature in Duke Forest's Blackwood Division. The "meadows" remained a common local term, as the 1918 *Soil Survey of Orange County* noted that about two square miles between Blackwood and Balls Mountains (present-day Bald Mountain, also located in the Blackwood Division) contained "natural prairie" and that when "Hillsboro was first settled the farmers each year came down to the area now known as the 'Big Meadows' and cut and cured hay from the native grasses. Since then the area has grown up to forest."

This Indenture, Made the *Fourteenth* Day of *March* in the Year of our Lord One Thousand Seven Hundred and *Fifty Five* and in the *xxiiii* Year of the Reign of our Sovereign Lord G E O R G E Second, by the Grace of God, of *Great-Britain, France,* and *Ireland,* King, Defender of the Faith *&c.* BETWEEN the Right Honourable *John Earl Granville,* Viscount *Carteret,* and Baron *Carteret,* of *Hawns,* in the County of *Bafford,* in the Kingdom of *Great-Britain,* Lord Prefident of His Majesty's Most Honourable Privy Council, and Knight of the Most Noble Order of the Garter, of the One Part, and *William Blackwood of Orange County in the Province of North Carolina, Planter* of the Other Part. W H E R E A S His said Most Excellent Majesty King G E O R G E the Second, in and by a certain Indenture, bearing Date the Seventeenth Day of *September,* in the Eighteenth Year of his Reign, and in the Year of our Christ One Thousand Seven Hundred and Forty Four, and made between his said Most Excellent Majesty of the one Part, and the said *John Earl Granville,* by the Name, Stile, and Title of the Right Honourable *John Lord Carteret,* of the other Part; D I D, for the Considerations therein mentioned, Give and Grant, Releafe, Ratify and Confirm, unto the said Earl, (by the Name of *John Lord Carteret,*) and his Heirs and Affigns, for ever, a certain Diftrict, Territory, or Parcel of Land; in the Province of *North-Carolina,* in *America,* and all the Sounds, Creeks, Havens, Ports, Rivers, Streams, and other Royalties, Franchifes, Privileges, and Immunities, within the fame, as they are therein fet out, allotted and granted, and confirmed, to the said *John Earl Granville,* by the Name of One Eighth Part of the Provinces of *South* and *North-Carolina;* as by the said Indenture, duly Enrolled in the High Court of Chancery in *Great-Britain,* and in the Secretary's Office of the Province of *North-Carolina,* Relation being thereunto had, will, amongst other Things, more fully and at large appear. N O W T H I S I N D E N T U R E W I T N E S S E T H, That as well for and in Confideration of the Sum of Three Shillings, Proclamation Money, to the said *John Earl Granville,* in Hand paid by the said *William Blackwood* at or before the Enfealing and Delivery of thefe Prefents, the Receipt whereof he the said Earl doth hereby acknowledge; as alfo, for and in Confideration of the Rents, Covenants, Exceptions, Provifoes, and Agreements, herein after-mentioned, referved, and contained, and by, and on the Part and Behalf of the said *William Blackwood, his* Heirs and Affigns, to be paid, performed, obferved, and kept; he the said Earl, H A T H given, granted, bargained, sold, and confirmed, and by thefe Prefents, D O T H, from himfelf, and his Heirs, give, grant, bargain, fell, and confirm, unto the said *William Blackwood, his* Heirs and Affigns, for ever, all that Piece and Parcel of Land, fituate, lying, and being in the Parifh of *St Matthews* and County of *Orange* in the Province of *North-Carolina,* in *America. On both fides*

Buffalo creeks, Beginning at a Black Oak, this North fide the creek; thence runing East 80 Ch. to a Black Oak; thence South crofsing Buffalo creek, 60 Ch. to a Spanish Oak, and a White Oak, thence West 80 Ch. to a Spanish Oak near the Buffalo creek; thence North crofsing Buffalo creek, 60 Ch. to the first Station;

Containing in the Whole, *Four Hundred & Eighty* Acres of Land: All which Premifes are more particularly defcribed and fet forth in the Plan or Map thereof hereunto annexed; together with all Woods, Underwoods, Timber, and Timber-Trees, Lakes, Ponds, Fifhings, Waters, Water-Courfes, Profits, Commodities, Appurtenances, and Hereditaments whatfoever thereunto belonging, or in any-wife appertaining, together with the Privilege of Hunting, Hawking, and Fowling, and of taking, catching, and making Ufe of all Sorts of Game in and upon the Premifes hereby granted, and all Mines and Minerals whatfoever therein to be found, except, and always referved out of this prefent Grant unto the King's Most Excellent Majefly, his Heirs and Succeffors, one Fourth Part of all the Gold and Silver Mines to be found in or upon the Premifes; and alfo except, and referved thereout, unto the said *John Earl Granville,* his Heirs and Affigns, one Moiety or half Part of the remaining Three Fourths of all fuch Gold and Silver Mines as fhall be found in or upon the said Premifes: T O H A V E A N D T O H O L D the said Piece or Parcel of Land, and all and fingular other the Premifes hereby granted, with the Appurtenances, (except as before excepted,) unto the said *William Blackwood, his* Heirs and Affigns, for ever, Y I E L D I N G A N D P A Y I N G therefore Yearly, and every Year, for ever, unto the said Earl, his Heirs and Affigns, the Yearly Rent or Sum of *Nineteen Shillings & two pence half penny* which is at the Rate of Three Shillings Sterling, or Four Shillings Proclamation Money, for every Hundred Acres, at or upon the Two moft ufual Feafts or Days of Payment in the Year, that is to fay, the Feaft of the Annunciation of the blefsed Virgin *Mary,* and the Feaft of St. *Michael* the Archangel, by even and equal Portions, and to be paid at the Court-houfe of the County of *Orange* aforefaid, unto the said Earl, or his Deputy-Attorney, or Receiver; for the Time being; the firft Payment thereof to be made on fuch of the said Feaft-Days, as fhall firft happen after the Date hereof. And the said *William Blackwood,* for himfelf, his Heirs and Affigns, and for every of them, doth hereby covenant, promife, and agree, to and with the said Earl, his Heirs and Affigns, and to and with every of them, by thefe Prefents, in Manner and Form following: That is to fay; That *he* the said *William Blackwood, his* Heirs and Affigns, fhall and will, Yearly, and every Year, for ever, well and truly pay or caufe to be paid unto the said Earl, his Heirs and Affigns, or unto his or their Deputy-Attorney, or Receiver, for the Time being, on the Days, and at the Place aforefaid, the aforefaid Yearly Rent or Sum of *Nineteen Shillings & two pence half penny* by half Yearly Payments, as aforefaid: And further, that *he* the said *William Blackwood, his* Heirs or Affigns, or fome or one of them, fhall and will, within Three Years, to be accounted from the Day of the Date hereof, clear and cultivate, at the Rate of Three Acres for every Hundred Acres, of the said Premifes hereby granted. P R O V I D E D always, and it is hereby exprefsly Declared and Agreed, by and between the said Parties hereunto, That if it fhall happen that the said Yearly Rent of *Nineteen Shillings & two pence half penny* or any Part thereof, fhall, at any Time hereafter, be behind or unpaid by the Space of Twenty One Days, next over or after any of the said Feaft-Days before limited or appointed for Payment thereof, and no fufficient Diftrefs can be found on the Premifes to levy fuch Rent and Arrears, with the Charges of Diftrefs;) or if the said *William Blackwood, his* Heirs or Affigns, fhall not within the Space of Three Years, after the Date hereof, clear and cultivate the Lands above granted, according to the Proportion of Three Acres for every Hundred; That then, and in either of the said Cafes, this prefent Grant, and all Affignments thereof, fhall be utterly void and of none Effect; and it fhall be lawful for the said Earl, his Heirs or Affigns, to regrant the fame to any other Perfon or Perfons whomfoever, as if this Grant, or any Affignment thereof, had never been made. I N W I T N E S S whereof, the Parties above-named have hereunto fet their Hands and Seals, the Day and Year firft above written.

Signed, Sealed, and Delivered, }
in the Prefence of Us, }

Wilm Blackwood

J ulia Blackwood's husband, Eugene, was born on the farm that borders the Blackwood Division of the Duke Forest and lived there all his life. The farm is part of a land grant to William Blackwood, dating to the mid-1700s. Julia recently sold the property to Orange County to be preserved as open space. Eugene and Julia's land is next to the Orange County Landfill, and they were heavily involved, with their neighbors, in discussions with Orange County regarding expansion of the county landfill.

Julia Blackwood, August 3, 2006. Photo by Judson Edeburn.

Settling the Land

These hardy, self-sufficient yeoman farmers worked with their hands and primitive tools to build one-room log houses, clear and burn the forests for farm and pasture land, and plant their crops. Living as they did in a landlocked region with primitive roads, they were unable to transport their crops to market, so they tended to be subsistence farmers, growing peas, beans, corn, wheat, and potatoes on small properties. According to Randy Daniel, "During the last half of the 18th century more than 75 percent of property owners [in Orange County] held between 40 and 200 hectares (100–500 acres); only 5 percent of the land owners held more than 405 hectares (1,000 acres)."

Only farmers with holdings over 500 acres in size and a large labor force comprised of family members or slaves had the manpower to grow labor-intensive crops such as tobacco and cotton. Most Piedmont landowners lacked such a labor force: the slave population in North Carolina's Piedmont region was smaller than that of the large plantations of the Coastal Plain. According to Kenzer, in 1755, 8 percent of the white families in Orange County owned slaves. By 1860, 33 percent of the Orange County population was African American, and the majority of these people were held as slaves.

"My grandfather used to keep hunting dogs for Ben Duke when he was a young man, and they'd come out here to what they called the Duke Farm, which was originally owned by the Strayhorns."

– Bob Strayhorn, descendant of Gilbert Strayhorn

Families supported each other through tightknit communities that often centered on the neighborhood church. As families expanded, new generations tended to settle near their parents, and marriage between cousins was customary. Neighborhoods organized around these clans developed throughout Orange County and assumed the names of the prominent family or natural feature, including the New Hope, Eno, Cane Creek, White Cross, and Patterson neighborhoods.

The colonists widened historical trade routes and game trails, expanding the road network and enabling wagon trade with distant communities such as Fayetteville and Petersburg, Virginia, that were gateways to seaports. Road intersections and river fords attracted businesses such as general stores, post offices, and gristmills. The enterprises often became the nexus of the neighborhood, where people gathered to socialize, gossip, and barter.

B.N. DUKE FARM.
ORANGE COUNTY, N.C.
1-INCH = 400 FT.

SUBDIVIDED BY
ATLANTIC COAST REALTY CO
PETERSBURG VA — GREENVILLE N.C.

A 1909 survey plat showing the B. N. Duke Farm, a portion of which is contained in the Eno Division of the Duke Forest. Office of the Duke Forest.

Mill Culture in Duke Forest

Before the adoption of steam power after the Civil War, colonists depended upon water-powered mills to grind their household wheat and corn and process wheat into flour to be sold at market. While not as extensive or storied as the mills that historically supported communities along the Eno River, several mills on New Hope Creek once sustained a lively mill culture.

"Mills played more than an industrial and economic role in the building of that early society. They played a social role as well, offering isolated families a place to meet their neighbors and to exchange news, opinions, encouragement, and information, and where they could hear the harangues of county politicians and list their taxables with the sheriff's constables. The millpond offered a swimming and fishing hole to the men and boys, and the thunder of the intricate machinery and glorious rush of water over the wheel added wonder and pleasure to their flat, work-ridden lives."

– Jean Bradley Anderson, *Durham County*

Remains of the Patterson mill dam, Korstian Division, along New Hope Creek. Photo by Ida Phillips Lynch.

Downstream from the sandstone bluffs of Hollow Rock, you can see remnants of the Patterson mill dam, an impressive 13-foot-high rock structure spanning more than 90 feet across the creek. A massive boulder looms over the creek and provides a base for one end of the dam about 300 feet upstream from Erwin Road. John Patterson, who immigrated to North Carolina from Maryland and Virginia, received a land grant for several parcels along this section of the creek in 1744, according to a history of the Patterson family by Mann Cabe Patterson. Patterson is thought to have operated the first gristmill on that reach of the creek and his family apparently maintained this enterprise in the future. According to a genealogy written by Hugh Conway Browning, in 1793, Mann Patterson, George Johnston, and Page Patterson obtained permission to build a gristmill and sawmill on New Hope Creek.

Choosing a successful mill site required an intimate understanding of the flow and topography of a stream. "A mill's location was an integral factor in its success or failure," writes Anderson. "It required first of all a site where bedrock could offer a secure footing for the mill foundation, preferably sufficiently high above the stream to escape the worst of the sudden flooding in Piedmont streams. Next it needed a site within a burgeoning farm population accessible by roads on both banks of the stream and by a good ford so that farmers could reach it from both sides."

New Hope Creek provided a few natural benefits for gristmills. The creek drops dramatically in the long descent down the edge of the Triassic Basin between N.C. Highway 86 and Erwin Road, and the rock outcrops that occur along the waterway were sturdy and well placed to anchor the dams. Patterson's mill was strategically located where the

"On Saturday last … we had a grand Pic-Nic party … if it will not tire you, I will endeavour to give you some idea, how a Pic-Nic party is conducted on Chapel Hill. The day was a very beautiful one, and about 9 o'clock all the vehicles which the village could boast were paraded in front of Miss Nancy's and after being almost filled with provisions, fishing rods, and the whole party including myself, mounted to our respective seats, and pre-ceeded by our fine College Band marched out of town. We found the roads to be in excellent order, and as was appointed, we drove out to the Mill, some five miles off, belonging to a Mrs. Patterson. When we reached there, all commenced fishing, but finding but little sport in practicing the 'angling art,' we adjourned to the Mill-House, where a dance was got up, and continued until we received the order from Miss Nancy to come to dinner. The table was spread under some large trees by the bank of the creek, and spread with 'eatables.' … The exercise we had taken gave us fine appetites, and we did full justice to the good things set before us.… The day, upon the whole, was a very pleasant one, and as such things are rather unusual here, will no doubt be long remembered by both young and old."

Hollow Rock along New Hope Creek. Photo by Ida Phillips Lynch.

– Letter from Rufus L. Patterson to Samuel F. Patterson, April 18, 1849, in the Jones and Patterson Family Papers #578, Southern Historical Collection, Wilson Library, The University of North Carolina at Chapel Hill

precolonial New Hope Road forded New Hope Creek (at the present-day Erwin Road bridge over the creek)—"on the 'shore line' of the Triassic Basin," remarks David Southern.

"Mill owners were the leading lights of their day," says Southern. "They were the most prominent people in a community because building a mill required capital for building and buying equipment like millstones. The Patterson Mill seat became a major community center, with a post office." Mann Patterson's grandson, Samuel F. Patterson, built a general store in the Patterson neighborhood in 1875;

it was the predecessor of two other general stores and community centers in the area, Trice's Store and the Hollow Rock Country Store.

Robson Mill

George Johnston sold a 143-acre property, including a grist and merchant mill, to William and Edward Robson in 1811. The Robson family operated the gristmill near the present-day Wooden Bridge for more than 60 years, but today the remnants of this enterprise are slowly sinking into the earth. In late April, jack-in-the-pulpit covers the red clay of the foundation and, rather than the hum of machinery, one hears the exuberant calls of oven-birds and other songbirds. Sections of the reddish-blue stone walls of the two-story millhouse are still standing. The hollowed-out headrace, the channel that carries the water that turned the mill wheel, is still intact, although trees and shrubs are growing in the channel and on the retaining wall. The tailrace, which returned the diverted water to the creek, is also visible.

Jack-in-the-pulpit (Arisaema triphyllum) *at the Robson Mill site. Photo by Ida Phillips Lynch.*

The Robsons were enterprising stoneworkers who built scores of stone walls that persist to this day, leading David Southern to dub them "lithomaniacs." The late Glenn Whitfield, whose family settled in the area around Whitfield Road in the 18th century, recalled in a 1994 interview that "back in those days, instead of fencing up a piece of land for cow pasture, everyone just let their livestock range the country. And a man had a brand, like out West. So Robson and Johnston [a neighboring miller] gathered stones from out of the field and used them to build rock fences that kept the cattle out of his field."

The Robsons sold their property to Robert Sharp in 1873. Erwin Cotton Mills purchased the land in 1925, and Duke University acquired it soon afterward, in 1927. Today the Johnston mill is protected in a Triangle Land Conservancy preserve upstream from the Robson mill.

Mill culture in the Piedmont thrived into the late 1800s. In 1860 "nearly half of the county's [Orange] manufacturing firms were mills that ground the locally grown corn and wheat," according to Robert Kenzer. Some of the mills along New Hope Creek likely operated until the early 20th century, but three factors caused their demise: the development of

Robson family cemetery. The periwinkle (Vinca minor) *ground cover shown here has now been replaced with the invasive Japanese stilt grass* (Microstegium vimineum). *Photo by Judson Edeburn.*

steam power enabled mills to move into growing industrial centers like Durham, sediment built up in the waterways, and devastating floods in the late 1800s and early 1900s washed away many dams and millponds.

The stone foundation of the Robson family homeplace lies uphill from the creek in a bramble of briars and saplings. The family cemetery is tucked into the woods beneath a few gnarled cedars about a quarter mile from the mill site. Three marked fieldstones weather under a mat of periwinkle and a recent invader, *Microstegium vimineum*. The inscriptions on the headstones memorialize these hard-working settlers, and give some indication of the lives they led:

Ann Robson
Wife of Wm. Robson
Born September 22, 1795
Decd. Feb. 7, 1872

William (Wm.) Robson
Born Royal Oak, England
May 25, 1783
Dec'd 4 April 1871

Memory of John Robson
Dcd. June 28 1842
Agd. 23 yrs

Hartford Mill Complex

The bustling Hartford Mill Complex was, according to the late historian Mary Claire Engstrom, historically located in the present-day Hillsboro Division along the Eno River. In 1978, Engstrom presented the first formal history of this sizeable mill complex at a seminar on waterwheels and windmills, held in conjunction with the bicentennial of the West Point on the Eno Mill.

Engstrom determined that the complex was located on the west bank of the Eno, where U.S. 70 crosses the river. In 1755, a Quaker miller named Joseph Maddock and his apprentice John Frazier built the original mill, not far downstream from the mouth of McGowan's Creek. By 1768, the property had been sold to Thomas Hart. Engstrom wrote that "the genial, gregarious Hart was a daring land speculator and a born gambler who delighted in taking long chances." Hart's mill soon became a seedbed for other enterprises. According to Engstrom, "Maddocks' old grist mill under its new owner became the nucleus for a sizeable village of 'Mills Manufactories, &c,' as Hart called them—a saw mill, an oil mill, a fulling mill, a distillery with two large stills, a weaving house, a tan-yard from which wagons regularly took loads of shoes into Hillsborough, plus a veritable army of skilled workmen, both black and white: carpenters, painters, brickmasons, tanners, cobblers, smiths, weavers, and so on."

The 1779 tax records indicate that Thomas Hart was the richest man in Orange County. But the following year he left the area, probably for political reasons. By 1782 Jesse Benton had taken over ownership of the mill complex. His son, the future senator Thomas Hart Benton, was born the same year. Jesse Benton died in 1790, and the plantation and complex were dissolved upon his death. Today, few traces of this thriving industrial center remain.

Tom Magnuson (on right) of the Trading Path Association has searched this area of Orange County extensively for evidence of the Hartford Mill and the Hart and Benton families. Duke Forest Photo Collection.

Changing Land Use Patterns

Until the Reconstruction, the greatest agent of change in the landscape was farming. Prior to the Civil War, most Orange and Durham County residents scratched out a living by growing corn, tobacco, and wheat. An inferior road system continued to plague the region and hinder the marketing of crops until the advent of a good roads campaign in the early 1900s. The stories of two families that lived in the Blackwood and Durham Divisions of the Forest illustrate typical farm life in the area and reveal how farmers' agricultural and land management practices produced the infertile farmland that became Duke Forest.

Farming in the Blackwood Division

To an untrained eye, the significance of the antebellum Hogan Plantation is not immediately apparent. The word "plantation" conjures a certain visual image that is incongruous with the scanty remnants of this farm. But archaeologists believe that the site contains significant information about the lives of enslaved African-Americans prior to the Civil War.

Alexander Hogan established a 380-acre plantation near present-day Eubanks Road in Chapel Hill in 1838. According to Randy Daniel, who helped nominate the Hogan property to the National Register of Historic Places, "The land had been in the family since the 1700s. . . . Wheat, corn, oats, and barley were the primary plantation crops."

Hogan married Matilda Robson in 1854, and they had eight children. By the end of the 1850s, Hogan had 13 young slaves working on his farm. Matilda inherited the farm when Alexander died in 1872, and when she died around 1890, the surviving children inherited the farm and sold part of the property to the Hogans' former slaves. The late Essie Leak, whose ancestors lived and worked on the Hogan Plantation, lived near the farm her entire life, and recalled the Hogan house as a two-story wooden plank house.

Essie Hogan Leak (center, in blue), great-granddaughter of Alexander Hogan, at the ceremony of the National Register of Historic Places registration of the Alexander Hogan Plantation Archeological Site, 1996. Duke Forest Photo Collection.

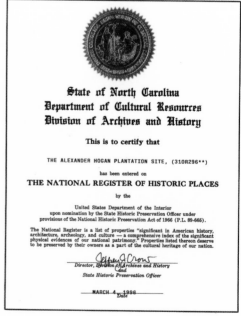

The Hogan Plantation Archeological Site, Orange County, was placed on the National Register of Historic Places in March 1996. Office of the Duke Forest.

Ghost Roads

The ghost roads of Duke Forest mark the routes of wagon and trading paths. These dim hollowed-out depressions are found throughout the woodlands and often parallel existing modern roads.

The New Hope Road

This precolonial road is a principal tributary of the Great Trading Path, and its gist corresponds loosely to a section of present U.S. 15. A connector of ancient habitations—sites that would develop into Oxford, Chapel Hill, and Pittsboro—it traversed three major watersheds: Tar-Pamlico, Neuse, and Cape Fear. Broken sections of it exist today as city streets and county roads; more of it, now abandoned, may be discovered as deep gouges in woods and back yards. In some subdivisions, these eroded traces have been filled, packed, and smoothed-over to the surrounding level, and thus have been permanently erased from the landscape.

The cobblestone roadbed known as the Old Oxford Road, or New Hope Road, passes through the Duke Forest. Duke Forest Photo Collection.

The road is called University Road in many old deeds and plats. The Bennehans, Camerons, and other early trustees of the University of North Carolina, traveled this road to conduct university business. Later names in other locations are Old Oxford Road, Old Chapel Hill Road, Road to Petersburg, and Road to Chatham Courthouse, and all of these refer to a single, ancient path.

The road enters Duke Forest in the Durham Division, north of N.C. 751 and east of U.S. 15-501 Bypass, where a wonderful link has been perfectly maintained. This section of the road is unique because it is cobbled. Apparently an early owner of that tract decided to fix his section of the road in a way that would be permanent, and he succeeded. The cobbled section corresponds neatly with lines of old deeds and ends near another Duke Forest road. From there, the older track runs cross-country; on the other side of N.C. 751 it continues again as a Duke Forest trail of gravel and cinders to a bridge alongside the original ford of Mud Creek. At that point the track of New Hope Road veers from the maintained path and can be picked up intermittently, sometimes as fence lines beside fields.

South of where it crosses Cornwallis Road, the old road is evident in backyards and woods, and a piece of it is still used for farm vehicles within the Blaylock land. Very near the junction of Mount Sinai Road, its track merges with present Erwin Road, and it followed that loosely, from side to side, for about three-and-one-half miles to Old Oxford Road, just south of Weaver Dairy Road.

This section, for two hundred years, was Patterson territory. By tradition, the large white house at the intersection of Erwin and Whitfield roads contains a room or two from the original John Patterson cabin, the homesite marked "I. Paterson" on the 1770 Collet map. Among his descendants were Mann Patterson and John Tapley Patterson, and two early nineteenth-century plats mark the course of University Road through their lands on both sides of New Hope Creek. In addition, these plats demonstrate the junction with the important Hillsborough-Fayetteville stagecoach road, of which the unpaved portion of Cambridge road is a vestige. A large pit in Duke Forest alongside Erwin Road and near the sites of Trice's Store and Patterson's Mill marks this ancient junction.

– David Southern, from an unpublished essay

Today all that remains of this plantation are the stone foundations of four or five structures and a cemetery with unmarked fieldstones. Students from Elon University conducted a preliminary archaeological survey of the site in 1993, and Daniel and other archaeologists later examined the site, which was placed on the National Register of Historic Places in 1996.

Daniel sees great potential for future archaeological surveys of the site, because "it represents an example of a small nineteenth-century plantation that spanned the antebellum and postbellum occupation of Orange County. Virtually no archaeological work has been done on any such site in the county." In particular, he believes that the ruins could provide valuable clues about African American life of the time, since "Much of the black American role in plantation life—and early American history in general—is recorded in the archaeological record rather than the written one."

"It must have been 1975 that Bob Peet and I took William Niering, a distinguished senior ecologist, out into Duke Forest. We were walking in an area of the Korstian Division that has since been badly damaged by Hurricane Fran. We came upon a giant oak tree with big spreading branches and a bunch of little oak trees. This tree must have been three feet in diameter and near it was a row of red cedar, a lot of them dead, and Frank looked at that and said, 'Well this was an old pasture, and this oak tree was in the middle of pasture. The red cedar was where the fence line had been, because birds would sit on the fence and defecate the cedar seeds.' He looked at the landscape and could tell a story about that place and the lives of people that once lived here. And I was amazed. I had always considered that having to deal with human effects was a negative thing—but at that moment I realized that in fact in order to study nature you also have to study people. People's lives are intertwined with the landscape. There are very few places where you can go in North Carolina that have not been touched by human hands."

– Norman L. Christensen Jr., 2006

The Couch Family Farm

The record of one Orange County farming family provides a meaningful illustration of farm life in land now managed as Duke Forest. In 1984, Duke University student Rachel Frankel tackled an ambitious thesis project for an honors history class: writing the biography of the land owned by the Thomas Couch family.

Frankel's thesis examined how five generations of a family used a piece of land near Piney Mountain Creek from 1750 to 1950 in the present-day Durham Division. While many historians have documented the archetypal southern plantation, Frankel profiled a small southern farm. Her research examined how popular farming methods contributed to the abandonment of the farm after the Civil War, a pattern repeated on small farms throughout the region.

Frankel recalls how her inaugural visit to the Couch farm seized her imagination: "At the suggestion of Syd Nathans, director of the seminar, I went to the farm with Norm Christensen. I had never walked through the woods with a botanist, nor had I thought about the history of land use. When Norm talked in one sentence about the Couches, patterns of land use, and forest growth, this uniquely complex history unfolded, and suddenly the forest was dynamic in ways I had never considered. When we walked into this old broken-down house and found these old letters sticking out of the floorboards, it just became irresistibly intriguing to me."

By studying primary sources such as the Couch family's estate papers, deeds, property plats, wills, and letters, as well as interviewing surviving family members, Frankel wove an intricate tapestry that examined "the possibilities and the limits of certain agricultural practices and the intelligent yet doomed approach to land-use the Couches chose," writes Frankel.

The Couch family's story in North Carolina began in 1754, when Thomas Couch received a 300-acre land grant near Piney Mountain Creek. This Scotch-Irish farmer had left Virginia in 1739 in search of better farm land after his Virginia holdings had become barren. Frankel explains that the size of Couch's land grant influenced how he chose to manage his new property: "His land was so abundant that, as land became exhausted by eighteenth-century farming practices, he could afford to clear new ground. . . . Thomas did not have to waste his precious labor and capital resources on low-yielding land. . . . The most intelligent choice was to produce the greatest yields with the smallest amount of capital and land."

Couch initially planted small areas of corn for cornmeal and hominy and supplemented the family's table by hunting, growing a vegetable garden, and fishing in New Hope and Piney Mountain Creeks. He transported his winter wheat to Robson's Mill for grinding. As the village of Hillsborough (then spelled Hillsboro) grew, Couch took pork, grains, and some dairy products to market, where he probably sold them by bartering. Couch was fortunate that the old Hillsboro-Fayetteville road ran through his property, making it easier for him to travel to the market by wagon.

Couch followed a pattern of "shifting-field agriculture" that involved farming a field until it became unproductive, abandoning the field, and clearing more woodland to plant a new crop. These agricultural practices were widespread among southeastern farmers at the time. "Prior to the USA's Civil War in the 1860s, agricultural fields were mainly derived from newly cleared forest, from 'fresh soil,'" write Daniel Richter and Daniel Markewitz in their book *Understanding Soil Change.* "After the soil's productive capacity began to decline, land was abandoned. After several years of a forest fallow, the old fields may have been brought back into cultivation by re-clearing and burning, which at least temporarily regenerated nutrient availability."

Thomas Couch Jr. inherited his father's property by the turn of the century. Between 1790 and 1823 he purchased additional land, including frontage along Piney Mountain Creek, so that by 1823 the farm comprised 1,600 acres and would have been considered a small plantation. The additional land made it even easier to shift crops around the property.

In some parts of the Forest, only gentle depressions remain where old roadbeds once crossed the landscape. Photo by Ida Phillips Lynch.

In 1850, William Couch Jr. was managing the bulk of the family farm, following his father's farming practices. "William cleared woodland in order to provide fresh ground for growing crops and left the exhausted fields empty to grow wild grasses for grazing his livestock," writes Frankel. "William was also loyal to traditional methods of cultivation. He did not terrace his fields nor did he build hillside ditches.... Rather, [he] continued to encourage soil erosion by sowing and reaping his crops up and down the slopes and hillsides." Frankel concluded that William Couch followed these traditional farming methods because he had an ample land base and lacked the resources and transportation to purchase fertilizer.

Even as agricultural reformers like Edward Ruffin introduced soil conservation strategies to the Southeast, many farmers disregarded these practices, causing great consternation among the more enlightened farmers. Frankel writes that in the mid-19th century, Orange County farmer J. W. Norwood spoke to fellow farmers and lamented their poor farming practices, saying that "all three of our great natural laws of agriculture have been disregarded and violated." Norwood chastised the farmers for not rotating crops, preventing soil erosion, or using fertilizer and asked them to "behold the melancholy consequence of such a system of cultivation in the exhausted and worn-out condition of our lands, as of this moment they lie spread out before us to our view."

The farm passed to William's sons upon his death. In 1861, John W. and William Couch Jr. left the farm to fight in the Civil War. In their absence much of the farm was left untouched and may have had time to recover, but in the aftermath of the war, they returned to a land where "nearly all farmers in the southeastern USA, black and white, faced almost insurmountable operational problems," write Richter and Markewitz. "Communities were decimated. Nearly four million African-Americans had been freed from slavery, yet few owned land, animals, or farm implements.... Agricultural statistics

of the 1870 Census illustrate a region that was crippled, poor, and not likely to move ahead rapidly."

In this unsettled environment the historic makeup of the traditional family farm began to unravel. "Farm abandonment was very rapid in the 1920s. In the 1930s social scientists considered soil exhaustion a major player in farm abandonment, but I think when we look back now we know it was part of a much bigger picture. After the Civil War, many family-owned farms were divided into smaller farms and tenant farming and sharecropping developed," says Richter. Fertilizers became commercially available, cotton growing began to expand in the western United States and compete with the southern market, and people moved to cities like Durham to work in factories.

By the early 20th century, work opportunities in industrial cities such as Durham lured many young farmers away from the family property. When John W. Couch died in 1917, his will divided his 300-acre property between his four children: J. W. T. Couch, Nettie Couch, Jennie Cate, and Hibernia Couch. "JWT," the last person to farm the property, moved his 11-member family to Durham in 1920, leaving Nettie Couch as the only family member residing on the property. Nettie Couch survived by selling her handmade quilts and renting part of her property to tenant farmers. But tenant farming was an unreliable source of income and by the time Duke University offered to purchase the Couch property in 1947, the family was willing to sell. Through a life estate, Duke allowed Nettie to continue living on the property until her death and the University ran a power line to her house, which until then had never had electricity.

The lessons from this landscape study remain with Rachel Frankel today. Now the owner of an architectural firm in New York City, Frankel believes that the experience sharpened her vision. "I learned how to look at a landscape and understand it, and that is invaluable to me," she says. "And I learned how to associate generic information like maps and censuses with human history. A lot of my architectural work is in an urban context, so being able to understand what's right under your feet illuminates it."

One dilapidated, white wooden house remains on the Couch property today, next to the fire trail. The house has no doors, and the beaded board interior walls are faded and buckling. The original Couch homesite lies uphill from that house, past a tributary of Piney Mountain Creek that may have provided the Couches with drinking water. Half-hidden on a knoll amid a tangle of wisteria are remnants of the roofing and part of the foundation of the original postbellum house, which had burned to the ground in the late 1980s. I visited it in the company of Duke Forest manager, Judd Edeburn, and Leanora Minai, a writer in the Duke University Communications Department, in July of 2006. Not far from the house site, we could make out the wooden walls of a structure, which turned out to be an intact, solidly built storage shed that may have once held grain or tools.

Edeburn pulled a nail out of the wall and showed it to us—it was a square "cut nail," he said, one that an archaeologist could use to date the building.

Near the house site, we walked through a grove of 70-year-old loblolly pines on a slope above the little stream. Knee-high oak and tulip poplar seedlings, mushrooms, and partridge berry dotted the brown pine straw underfoot. Edeburn pointed out the corrugated pattern in the ground: the ridges and furrows of the Couch family's farming operation. Some of the rows were plowed uphill, which would have caused the soil to wash away into the creek. Standing under the trees it was hard to imagine that not that long ago—80 years or so—this shady pine stand was an open cotton or tobacco field. "Just think about all the effort the Couch family must have expended to clear this field, and now it's completely overgrown," remarks Edeburn. "This is one of the basic lessons Duke Forest teaches us, every day—how quickly nature can overtake human endeavors."

All that remains of the Nettie Couch house. Lightning likely struck the abandoned home in the late 1980s. Duke Forest Photo Collection.

Chapter 4
A School Grows with the Forest

"I WILL BE VERY GLAD INDEED to confer with you about what we should do with some of the forests we have purchased. I hope that we may be able to give a course in forestry. Of course this will be some time in the future. We have purchased about four thousand acres of land, some of which is in virgin forests. We need some expert advice. If you do come to Durham in the near future, I will be very glad to confer with you. . . . I really would like to show you some of our forests."

– From a letter from R. L. Flowers (vice president of Trinity College) to J. S. Holmes (North Carolina state forester), November 7, 1925

"Other universities have their institutes of human relations and social research and special laboratories in the sciences that give them outstanding significance, but none of them is surrounded by a forest which offers anything like the possibilities offered by the Duke Forest."

– Committee on Forestry, Duke University Board of Trustees, June 5, 1933 (*Duke University Alumni Register 9*, June 1933)

Duke University's School of Forestry literally grew from the ground up. By late 1925, the University had amassed nearly 5,000 acres of forest and agricultural land west of the burgeoning campus, a swath of land that far exceeded the construction room needed for the expansion of Trinity College into Duke University. President William Few was faced with a decision: how should the university utilize this new property?

In 1921, when Few was president of Trinity College, he had presented James B. Duke with a proposal about the types of professional schools that could be housed at the new university. His recommendations at that time did not include a forestry school. "Both idealistic and practical considerations soon combined to suggest that Duke University put its vast forest to educational use," writes Durden in *The Launching of Duke University*. "On the idealistic side, Few, while certainly not alone among educational leaders in espousing generous service as his institution's principal reason for existing, possessed an unusually strong commitment to the idea of Duke University's being of as much help and value as possible to its state, region, and nation." The practical reasons were decidedly more pedestrian. "I think they became worried about tax liability because if the land was not put to educational uses they'd be liable for property taxes," says Durden.

Forestry professionals helped convince Few that the university's land holdings provided the perfect setting for a sorely needed forestry school in the South. The South of the 1920s, while rich in forestland—much of it second-growth pine forest that was overtaking abandoned fields—lacked a strong forestry school to promote the management of the changing landscape. Forest research and education were quite new in the United States: the Biltmore Forest School in Asheville, North Carolina, was the first forestry school in the United States; it had opened only in 1898, and the country's first undergraduate forestry curriculum had been introduced at Cornell University the same year.

The idea of creating a forestry school at Duke surfaced in a report that forester W. W. Ashe wrote for Duke University in May 1926, in which he provided management strategies for the Forest "in connection with a proposed school of forestry." A native North Carolinian, Ashe worked for the U.S. Forest Service and was instrumental in helping create national forests in the eastern United States. In his report, Ashe wrote that his "hurried and altogether superficial examination seems to show that the varied conditions and proximity to the University present an exceptional opportunity for development for forest demonstrational and forest experimental purposes." Ashe's advice would soon provide an invaluable roadmap for the building of a forestry school.

Nelson C. Brown, the acting dean of the New York State College of Forestry, wrote Few on May 5, 1927, saying: "There is no question but that the South has the greatest opportunity for forestry in the future, of any region in the country. There are millions of acres of land which must always remain in forests. The prosperity of the southern people is dependent, to a large degree, upon the permanence of its forest resources."

One month later, Brown wrote Few and told him that he had "consulted confidentially with Col. William B. Greeley, Chief of the U.S. Forest Service at Washington, and with a number of other leaders in forestry and they seem to be entirely unanimous in their approval of the establishment of a good strong school of forestry somewhere in the South." Brown enclosed a preliminary plan that outlined the need and general objectives for creating such a school at Duke University. He noted that most of the United States' 25 forestry schools were primarily in the North, Northwest, or Northeast, except for a handful in the South. He described the South as:

> the most important forest area in the United States from the standpoint of timber production. Of the 293 million acres of softwood forests in this country, 114 million, or about 40%, are in the South Atlantic, east Gulf and lower Mississippi regions. It is a region too, where forest devastation has gone farther than in any other locality, and today 34 million acres, ninety per cent of which is pine land, are classed by Federal foresters as non-productive.

Brown also suggested that North Carolina was favorably positioned for housing a forestry school, as forests covered more than two-thirds of the state and "the manufacture of timber products is the third largest industry in the state." E. H. Frothingham, the director of the Appalachian Forest Experiment Station in Asheville, also encouraged Few in a January 1930 letter, writing that his office was "immensely

Clarence F. Korstian. Duke University Archives.

interested in your plans for the school of forestry because we see in it powerful means for the development of the practice of forestry in the South."

At the urging of faculty in Duke's Botany Department, Few also solicited advice from Frothingham's colleague, Clarence Korstian, a senior silviculturist with the Forest Service who had received his doctorate in forestry from Yale in 1926 and was working in the North Carolina coastal plain in the late 1920s. "In one of our very early talks the late President Few, a Harvard graduate, suggested that we organize our program along the lines upon which the Harvard Forest was being operated," wrote Korstian in the 1963 issue of *Taeda* (the Duke School of Forestry yearbook and the Latin name for "resinous pines").

> Having previously visited the Harvard Forest and worked in the three Yale forests on two different cooperative research projects I felt reasonably qualified to discuss Dr. Few's suggestion. As Harvard did not have the proper emphasis on organized instruction in forestry as at Yale, I suggested that we carefully consider both the Harvard and Yale plans and then develop the Duke plan. In essence this meant completion of the mapping, forest inventory, and placing the Forest under a plan of sustained income from needed thinnings and harvest cuttings.

In a 1959 interview with Korstian conducted by Elwood R. Maunder, Korstian explained that he also suggested that "the Forest ought to be organized as a very definite adjunct to a graduate school of forestry" and "should serve the School of Forestry the way the hospital served the Medical School."

After that meeting, Few offered Korstian the position of the first director of the Forest. Korstian accepted: "The forest here was what really persuaded me to come down. I had been traveling three to six or seven hundred miles to get to some of my work on the coastal plains and I even had some work in Connecticut on two of my projects. . . . I decided that it was a real challenge here and that I should come down." On September 1, 1930, Korstian became the first director of the Duke Forest.

Other forestry professionals immediately praised Duke's foray into forestry. In the February 1931 issue of the *Journal of Forestry* editor-in-chief Emanuel Fritz wrote:

> Demonstration forests are sadly needed in every forest region of this country. It is not enough to know the basic sciences controlling tree growth and the silvicultural systems developed in Europe; the American forester needs more urgently, actual experience in applying his class-room knowledge. . . . American forestry schools, with several notable exceptions, are deplorably weak in forest laboratories. While some have acquired forests after their organization, others still evade the burden of an expensive demonstration area. Duke is unique in starting with a forest before it develops classrooms.

In an unpublished manuscript, "The Beginnings of an American University," Few wrote that Duke's property and its location in the Piedmont of North Carolina gave the institution

> an unusual opportunity to promote the cause of forestry. The protection and renewal of forests is fast becoming a live question in America. It has already been neglected too long. If we can help to stimulate an increasing interest in this vital question and render some actual service to the cause we shall thereby make a solid contribution to the welfare of this and future generations.

Early Forest Management

Korstian's vision about how to manage the Forest closely followed the suggestions outlined by Ashe's report. In the April 1932 *Bulletin of Duke University*, Korstian explained that the Forest would be managed as a place to demonstrate silvicultural practices, an "experimental forest for research into the problems of timber growing," and as an outdoor laboratory for field work. With the help of assistant director William Maughan, who joined the staff in January 1931, Korstian conducted a complete inventory of the Forest (or "growing stock") in order to develop a management plan. Through

this methodical inventory they divided the Forest into compartments and recorded the amount of timber, its history, composition, age, and approximate date of maturity.

First issue of The Duke Forest Bulletin, 1935. Office of the Duke Forest.

Ever the vigilant recordkeeper, Korstian amassed data in his first inventory that have proven to be immensely useful in forestry research. "Korstian's census of the forest stands in the Durham and Korstian Divisions is an amazing data set," says Norm Christensen. "Now we know what the forest composition, age, and tree density was in 1931."

Another of Korstian's early goals was to harvest trees, in part because he hoped that timber revenue could make the Forest financially self-sufficient and fiscally independent of the University. These harvesting practices continue to this day. As planted and natural tree stands reached maturity in the Forest, Korstian oversaw field crews and contract loggers that harvested the timber.

Korstian's strategy produced enough revenue that the "Duke Forest Fund financed the purchase of several pieces of land needed to round out the Forest

Loading logs along N.C. Highway 751, Durham Division, 1935. Photo by C. F. Korstian. Duke Forest Photo Collection.

boundaries," according to Korstian. "Clarence was a frugal man in many respects," writes Charles W. Ralston, former dean of the School of Forestry, in the spring 1983 issue of *FOREM*, the newsletter for Duke's School of Forestry and Environmental Studies:

> As director of the Duke Forest he always showed a goodly balance of income over expenses and had the authority to buy more forest land with the surplus. Duke Forest was a rural, operational forest during his tenure, and during World War II, with strong markets for pine saw timber and with no faculty or teaching duties, he managed to nearly double the size of the forest.

By 1948, the Forest encompassed 7,850 acres. In the 1959 interview with Maunder, Korstian said that at that time the Forest was "still self-supporting.... We made it pay right from the beginning, with one exception." (The exception was when the University paid the Forest $300 to finance a tree-planting operation.)

Korstian showed an entrepreneurial spirit in marketing the Forest's timber and other resources. In the April 1941 *Report*, he noted that during 1939 and 1940 the Forest crews had harvested and sold "180,000 feet of pine sawlogs, 11,000 feet of oak logs, 3,500 feet of red gum logs, 13,000 feet of red cedar logs for cedar chests and a little hickory and yellow poplar for a total of 208,000 board feet of sawtimber." Korstian

A two-acre clear-cut plot in Durham Division, Compartment 66, 1936. Wood is "penned" to dry before used for heating purposes. Photo by C. F. Korstian. Duke Forest Photo Collection.

Planting of an abandoned field in 1932, Durham Division, Compartment 72. The original black-and-white photo has been hand-tinted in color. Duke Forest Photo Collection.

The information provided in this early plantation record is typical of the detailed records kept by Dr. Korstian and his staff. Office of the Duke Forest.

"We started [loading logs] with a Studebaker and then we went to that GMC. We'd pull that cable underneath and hook it, and he dropped his load off. He'd pull the logs out of the way and I'd stand back there on the platform and winch it up. It'd turn around and we'd let the truck go by and I'd let them all down and I'd straighten them all up."

— Atlas Rigsbee, February 5, 2003

The R. L. Rigsbee Sawmill, along Farrington Road, south of Chapel Hill. Date unknown. Photo courtesy of Atlas Rigsbee.

"I suppose my daddy was one of the first to begin doing any logging for Duke University. I remember living over here at this old white house when Dr. Korstian and Professor Maughan came out and talked with my daddy and that was, in my mind, 1933. They asked my daddy if he'd be interested in coming over and doing some logging when necessary. He had cut some bridge timbers for anybody that needed it. Back then they used wood and bridge timbers and they cut for the city of Durham. They needed hard pine to go under the bridges. So he was interested. He went over there and brought a log cart and brought one log at a time from wherever it was over there to this place to be sawed.

J. A. Watson's sawmill, somewhere in the "New Hope Valley," 1935. Photo by C. F. Korstian. Duke Forest Photo Collection.

"Back then they used six-foot crosscut saws to log the trees. It would take two men about half a day to cut one tree. Of course you have to remember that trees swell at the butt. And remember the size of the trees at that time. It was called the virgin pine, and that's what my daddy needed.

"When my daddy first started, you had to cut the stump of the tree, no matter how big it was, flush with the ground, skin the stump, cover it up with dirt. When you felled the tree, you had to remove the cover of the stump, and the laps [had] to be laid flat to the ground. Now, that was the requirement."

— J. A. Watson Jr., August 1, 2002

also marketed what he described as "minor products" from the Forest, including "1,846 yards of sand from the creek bottoms." Judson Edeburn, the current resource manager of Duke Forest, recalls that the thrifty Korstian also saved the manure from a pasture in the Forest that was leased to a local farmer. "Who knows what he used it for?" says Edeburn.

Signs of the Times

Before some sections of the Forest could be harvested, Korstian and his staff had to work to reverse the devastating effects of erosion. "On a number of previously-cultivated fields the top-soil had been largely washed away and others were still in the process of degradation," Korstian wrote in his 1963 *Taeda* article. "In other cases deep gullies were moving toward important roads and, in at least one case, a very deep gulley was threatening a paved road. Much of this land was terraced with the assistance of U.S. Soil Conservation Service and Civilian Conservation Corps labor."

In May 1933, the Civilian Conservation Corps (CCC), whose formation Korstian described in the April 1935 *Report of the Director of the Duke Forest* as "one of the most significant developments along forestry lines that has ever taken place in this country," established 11 camps in North Carolina. The CCC was a work relief program developed as part of President Franklin D. Roosevelt's New Deal to combat the poverty and unemployment of the Great Depression; it provided unemployed men with work in various public works projects, including public and privately owned forests. Some of the 215 men who were based in a CCC camp near Durham helped construct over five miles of roads ("truck trails") in the Forest.

"I don't recall anybody using [machinery]—everybody used draft animals, a lot of people did. I could stray away from the subject and even up to the contemporary age I wish I had a good trained horse. To me it's where on earth would you [get somebody] to handle a horse. A lot of these younger people will probably want to know where the clutch was. A well-trained horse or mule, I've had both. I could just stand and look at them after they've been trained…it's just awesome how well they can perform.

"I made them [the horses] stay an hour after the log truck left. I dropped the tongs, then spoke to the horse and told him to get in the trailer and he did. And Joe said 'I see it I see it, but I don't believe it.' Well that was, in my opinion, was not the best-trained horse I had. Of anything I know of today, it is far superior to anything I know of today. And it depends a whole lot on the person managing the horse. If you got one man today and one man tomorrow, the horse can get confused."

– J. E. Booth, July 23, 2002

J. E. Booth at his home, August 6, 2006. Photo by Judson Edeburn. Duke Forest Photo Collection.

Gullies before erosion control work was undertaken. Durham Division, Compartment 5, 1934. Photo by C. F. Korstian. Duke Forest Photo Collection.

Check dams built by the Civilian Conservation Corps in a large gully in Durham Division, Compartment 5, 1934. Photo by C. F. Korstian. Duke Forest Photo Collection.

A tractor crew of the Civilian Conservation Corps putting in fill to bridge over a branch of Mud Creek on Gate 5, 1934. Photo by C. F. Korstian. Duke Forest Photo Collection.

As one of his cost-saving measures, Korstian arranged to use the Duke Chapel tower as a fire lookout station, noting that the tower provided a view of almost all of the Durham and New Hope Creek Divisions. In an article written for *FOREM*, Harold K. Steen wrote that although using the chapel as a fire lookout was "perhaps a bit ragtag," there were no big fires during this time, and that "in 1955 Korstian reported that Hurricane Hazel did more damage to the forest than a quarter-century of fire."

While bolstering the infrastructure of the Forest, Korstian also focused on replanting trees on former agricultural lands. Beginning in 1931, he and his staff initiated an annual planting regime in the Forest with the goal of "putting to economic use the depleted or otherwise submarginal farm lands and the old abandoned fields which are not restocking naturally to desirable forest trees," as he explained in the 1935 *Report*. Forest crews hand-planted thousands of seedlings, mainly loblolly pine, as well as yellow poplar, shortleaf pine, longleaf pine, black locust, and small experimental stands of bald cypress and red cedar. Korstian wrote in the April 1941 *Report* that as of that time, the staff had planted 811,000 trees in new plantations that comprised 814.25 acres.

The bridge over New Hope Creek between Compartments 16 and 19, New Hope Creek Division, built by the Civilian Conservation Corps, 1934. Photo by C. F. Korstian. Duke Forest Photo Collection.

A Day in the Field with Korstian

An article in the March 1931 issue of Duke's *Alumni Register* provides a glimpse of Korstian in the field. With an exuberant introduction that proclaimed, "A trip through the Duke forest is one never to be forgotten," the reporter described touring the Forest with a group in a two-car convoy. They traveled down then-unpaved Highway 751 and made numerous stops to photograph the Forest and discuss the efforts to reforest the depleted farm land.

At one of the reforestation plots, the writer described a landscape in disrepair: "There before the party lay what had been an abandoned tobacco field. The soil was worn out and useless for farm land. In the clearing stood a cabin, empty and forlorn, and rapidly falling into ruins." Korstian explained that in sites like this one, where trees were not reseeding on their own, the Forest staff was planting loblolly and other pine species. Korstian continued these reforestation efforts for many years and established the nucleus of the pine stands that today serve as research sites and sustain the daily operations of the Forest. (Today many areas are marked with brown hand-lettered signs that provide a chronology of the life of each plantation, from seeding to cutting, to prescribed burning, to regrowth.)

During the tour Korstian discussed his vision for managing the Forest and establishing what would become the first graduate forestry school in the South. At one point, he lingered on one of his pet subjects: the importance of understanding and protecting forest soils. Kneeling down, he scraped away the leaf litter and reflected on the diversity of life in the topsoil: "Much of this top layer is composed of decayed leaves and other vegetable matter. But it is fairly alive with animal life. See here—this little salamander, picking his way through the leaves. Here's the runway of a rodent. That's a field mouse or a shrew. If we sat down quietly here for a while, on a hot day, the whole place would be alive with sounds of the animal life—the spiders, the worms, the bugs, the rodents."

Duke woodland fireplace. One of the participants in a tour led by Dr. Korstian wrote this note of thanks: "Mr. Korstian, Just a note of appreciation of my pleasant day about the Duke Forest. Perhaps you noticed the article in the Raleigh morning paper about it. G. A. Crourie." April 1, 1933.

View of the Crow's Nest picnic site, showing a spring, and the trail, footbridge, and fence erected to keep horses from the spring. Durham Division, 1934. Photo by C. F. Korstian. Duke Forest Photo Collection.

Clearly moved by the visit to the Forest, the writer closed his article by describing the Forest as "so old, and yet so new, whose life is young, old, and middle-aged" and stated that he had "a feeling that perhaps they had been close to the heart of one of the greatest parts of this great institution."

"The red cedar plantation set out last year was enlarged this year by some 2,000 trees. Red cedar is a valuable commercial species as it can be used early in life for Christmas trees, a little later for posts, and as it matures, for poles and sawlogs. Cedar brings a price which is becoming more and more attractive owing to the rapidly diminishing supply of naturally established stands in the region."

– Clarence F. Korstian, *Report of the Dean of the School of Forestry: 1938-1939*, March 1940

Hand-loading cedar logs at the Funston siding, 1940. Photo by J. R. Jester. Duke Forest Photo Collection.

"Of special interest at this time in connection with the marketing program is the contribution that the Forest has recently been able to make in the interests of national defense. Faced with the need for rapid expansion in existing navy yards and defense radio facilities, the Government has placed large orders for extra long poles and piling material, and the companies which ordinarily supply this material have been hard pressed to locate and obtain the extra long timbers. Having some of this long material on hand, in the stand near the Crow's Nest, the Staff was willing to cooperate with the companies and get it out although the cutting of pine during the dry summer season was contrary to policy owing to the danger of infestation by bark beetles in the remaining trees. . . . It is understood that some of the long 80- and 90-foot poles from the Forest are to be used in constructing a large radio net or antennae at the United States Naval Academy at Annapolis Maryland, and that the long piling is going to the Norfolk and New London Navy Yards."

Loading poles for shipment to a treating plant in Wilmington, North Carolina, 1938. Photo by C. F. Korstian. Duke Forest Photo Collection.

– Clarence F. Korstian, *Report of the Dean of the School of Forestry: 1939-1940*, April 1941

Public Recreation in the Forest

Local residents, university students and faculty flocked to the Forest on outings almost immediately upon its establishment. In the April 1935 *Bulletin*, Korstian wrote that the five picnic sites in the Forest (each containing "a receptacle for refuse, and a stone fireplace constructed for cooking, either with or without utensils") had been used by 3,500 people in 1932–1933 and by more than 4,000 people in 1933–1934. He added that "the grounds are serviced once a week involving renewal of the wood supply and the disposition of garbage." More than 4,600 people hiked or rode horses along the Forest's fire trails the same year. The March 1940 *Bulletin* noted that 15,000 people visited the Forest in 1938–1939 and that the Gate 7 and Piney Mountain areas were the most popular picnic sites. The New Hope Division of the Forest housed a Boy Scout camp and a cabin for the Woman's Athletic Association of the Woman's College. And according to the *Bulletin*, the Durham City Hiking Club, the Explorers' Club, and biological clubs visited the Forest on organized outings.

The School of Forestry, along with the Duke Forest Office, was first located in the Biology Building on the Quadrangle next to Duke South Hospital. Duke Forest Photo Collection.

The Duke School of Forestry: Some Reminiscences

The Duke School of Forestry has evolved since its doors opened in 1938 into Nicholas School of the Environment and Earth Sciences (NSEES), but the students' and faculty's deep connection to Duke Forest has remained a constant over time. In September of 1938, 21 students enrolled in the new Duke School of Forestry under the guidance of Dean Korstian. It was among the first graduate-level forestry schools in the nation, after Yale University and Harvard University. The students came from 13 states, Canada, China, Japan, and the Dominican Republic. By this time Korstian had recruited an impressive staff comprised of some of the leading foresters and ecologists of the time.

The legacy of the founding faculty can be traced through their voluminous papers and records. What may not be as well-known are the lasting personal impressions that these instructors and researchers made on their students and colleagues: what they were like as people.

View of the Scoggins Mountain picnic site, from just west of main entrance road, facing east. Durham Division, Compartment 67, 1933. This picnic site is no longer used. Photo by C. F. Korstian. Duke Forest Photo Collection.

Clarence F. Korstian was dean, professor of forestry, and director of Duke Forest; his tenure at Duke lasted from 1931 to 1958. Charles W. Ralston, former dean of the School of Forestry, reminisced about Korstian in the spring 1983 issue of *FOREM*:

> [Korstian's] frugality at the personal level became apparent to me on occasions when I made field trips with him as a junior faculty member. We always departed (in a school car, of course) around 7 a.m., so that breakfast would be on the expense account. This account was meticulously recorded to the nearest penny in a little notebook that I suspected was a diary liberated from his Forest Service days.
>
> On one trip to the Green Swamp, we had stopped at a crossroads store for gas and saw an array of one-gallon buckets of gallberry honey on a dimly lit upper shelf. He instantly adopted his air of disinterested nonchalance that involved clasping his hands behind his back, rocking on his heels, and whistling tunelessly while rolling his eyes skyward. After a few moments of this routine, he offhandedly asked the shopkeeper what he "was getting for the honey." When, after the price was mentioned, Clarence said, "I believe I'll have four buckets," I assumed that this was a rare bargain and got one myself.

William Maughan was professor of forest management; he taught at Duke from 1931 to 1948. Of him, Ralston remarks:

> Clarence Korstian brought Bill Maughan to Duke as the first manager of Duke Forest. As such, he effected the first boundary surveys, timber type maps, volume inventories, and management plans for the forest. His work in the early 1930s included establishment of a grid of permanent sample plots for periodic reinventories. . . . He had a completely serious approach to his academic responsibilities and a dour look about him. His overall characteristics earned him the respectful dread of his students and his student alias, "Black Maughan."

Ralston's essay in *FOREM* includes also this pithy characterization of another member of the founding faculty, Albert E. Wackerman, who was professor of forest utilization from 1938 to 1967: "To me, Wack's outstanding characteristic was his unfailing optimistic approach to things. Repeatedly, he taught, 'There are no problems in forestry, only opportunities,' and he lived by this creed."

Early faculty of the School of Forestry. Top row, left to right: R. B. Thomson, W. Maughan, C. F. Korstian, A. E. Wackerman, and F. X. Schumacher. Front row, left to right: E. S. Harrar, F. A. Wolf, and P. J. Kramer. Photo by J. R. Jester. Duke Forest Photo Collection.

William Maughan, 1935. Maughan served as both assistant director of the Forest under Korstian and taught on the faculty of the School of Forestry. Photo by C. F. Korstian. Duke Forest Photo Collection.

Theodore S. Coile, professor of forest soils, and member of the faculty from 1932 to 1953, is recalled by Ralston as:

> a big man—physically and intellectually. He had a sort of John Wayne style and expressed his ideas with such conviction that a student would never doubt their validity. . . . His major contribution to forest soils research was development of soil-site techniques for evaluating forest productivity. When some of his peers questioned the validity of his empirical regression models, a typical reply was, "If the site index of loblolly pine were correlated with the number of squirrels per acre, then, . . . damn it, I'd count squirrels."

One of the first students at the new forestry school, Randy Boggess, graduated in May of 1940 and became a research forester at the Alabama Agricultural Experiment Station. Boggess was introduced to the Forest in field exercises in ecology taught by Henry J. Oosting and worked on a research project with Korstian in the summer of 1936, for a wage of 30 cents an hour. "The experience I had working on the Forest, and with various members of the faculty, was very valuable to me," recalls Boggess. "I have fond recollections of both the Forest and the people. My favorite spot in the Forest was

the 60–70-year-old loblolly pine stand behind Gate 7. In the following years, I never saw a better one. My least favorite was the New Hope Division, where, during my class in forest surveying, I became host to enough chiggers to last a lifetime."

"Mr. Blackmon [the superintendent of the Forest] usually came to the Forestry Office at 8 in the morning to discuss work plans with Bill Maughan. One morning, (it happened to be April 1st) Scotty Harrar came rushing into the office and said, 'Blackie, there is a fire down at the heating plant.' Mr. Blackmon took off in high gear and got all the way to the heating plant before he realized it was a big April Fool joke. He took it in good spirits and everyone had a good laugh."

– William R. (Randy) Boggess

Later students were equally impressed with the quality of both the school's faculty and outdoor facility. "I graduated from Rutgers University in the preforestry program in 1954 and our forestry class visited Duke in 1953 and went out into Duke Forest with Dr. Korstian," recalls Norm Brocard, a 1964 graduate of the Forestry School. "It was quite a pleasure for young foresters to walk in the footsteps of such a respected forestry leader. Dr. Korstian led us into a young sapling stand and asked the group: What should be done with a stand like this? We all gave some kind of a prescriptive silviculture remedy in order not to look completely ignorant. His answer? Do nothing here. And the lesson was to look at a stand of trees realistically, and leave it alone if it is doing what Mother Nature intended it should do."

Boyd Post, who received his master's in 1958 and a Ph.D. in 1962, says that his

Left to right: forest assistants Kenneth Carvell and Barry Malac, with Forest superintendent M. R. Blackmon, collecting tree diameters in 1953. Duke Forest Photo Collection.

favorite memories go back to the summer mensuration course that all incoming master of forestry students had to take. He remembers Professor F. X. Schumacher ("better known as 'Schu'") teaching the course "in his inimitable style": "During the first week, Schu was deriving a long, very complex equation at the blackboard and all the eager students were trying like crazy to keep up with him and make sense out of what he was saying as he rapidly filled up the board with all sorts of strange symbols and numbers. He was nearly to the bottom of the board when he stopped, looked at all the puzzled faces watching him and with a sly smile said, 'Aw, hell's bells—it's obvious!', and walked out of the room. We never revisited that material, even though we used the results in our mensuration procedures. Thank goodness we were never asked to repeat all that 'obvious' material on a test."

A silviculture class in 1950, under the direction of Dean Korstian (leaning over), studies Permanent Sample Plot 43 in the Durham Division. Photo by B. F. Smith. Duke Forest Photo Collection.

"There was honeysuckle all over the place and we had bush axes cutting it back. And the thing that impressed me more than anything else was the fact that it was hotter than hell and there were chiggers....I think Korstian stuck me out there with a bush ax to see if I really meant what I was saying that I really wanted to do forestry business."

– Sandy Davison, later superintendent under Korstian's successor, Lee Chaiken, recalling his first job at the Forest, when he was 15 years old.

Student Barry Malac using an alidade and plane table for surveying in the Duke Forest, 1952. Photo by K. L. Carvell. Duke Forest Photo Collection.

Tom Terry, a 1967 Forestry School graduate, recalls that while his class was "in awe of the excellent forestry faculty," the Forest "stands out even more as a lasting impression. The Forest was a living laboratory that formed the backdrop for so many lectures and class exercises. Rather than being stuck in an indoor class room, we could go the field and set up lab exercises for class. We were fortunate that the Forest was a working forest rather than a preserve or just an experimental forest or teaching laboratory. One impression that it left on everyone was that you could manage a forest and retain the economic, recreational, and environmental values."

In 1953, after Fred White graduated from the School of Forestry, he was appointed superintendent of the Forest, under Professor Lee Chaiken, Korstian's successor, following the retirement of M. R. (Manley) Blackmon. He recalls his predecessor as superintendent vividly: "Blackmon—as much as anyone I've ever known to be—was belligerent. I remember one afternoon when he was just totally fed up with everything. He ripped his hat off and threw it on the ground, and jumped up and down on it. He had the vocabulary of six sailors rolled into one. The crew just stood there, let it blow its course, then one of them reached down and picked up his hat, dusted it off, and handed it to him."

White would visit Blackmon long after the older man retired. They would sit on the front porch and drink a "clandestine beer," recalls White, "because his wife didn't approve. And he would spin tales about building the Chapel and his connections through that. And talk about all the

"Near Mt. Sinai, there was a still in there. I was working part-time for the Forest while I was in school, and fellow student Bill Hawkins and I found that still. And we watched it with the idea we would walk in about the time they were running it. You know, it was a nice size still down at that little creek. And we were sitting up there in the woods one night and, sure enough, here come the guys that are going to run it. They tip-toed down in there to get started. Bill and I sat up on that hill to watch them. They got all set up and they were just getting ready to go and we were going to move in on them and chase them out and act like revenuers, and here comes a damn ABC officer down the bank on the other side. We were just about in the still when that happened. We ran like hell."

– Sandy Davison, on an incident that occurred while he was a student at the Duke School of Forestry

bad things I was doing on the Forest." Blackmon, in White's view, was "all business."

White remembers his colleagues with affection. "The crew that I had, they were just sheer fun. Pickle (Will Reid) was an institution. He was a huge man. I remember one day when they had to change a tire from the station wagon that I drove. They couldn't find the jack so Pickle picked up the end of it and set it on a block, changed the tire and picked it up and set it down again."

White succeeded Chaiken as director of the Forest, while E. S. (Scotty) Harrar was dean of the School of Forestry. As a member of the faculty, teaching measurement, dendrology, and other subjects, White was considered by his students to be one of the best teachers they had ever studied under.

M. R. Blackmon is pictured on the right with a 1950 silviculture class observing disking for hardwood control. Photo by B. F. Smith. Duke Forest Photo Collection.

"**I** was working with Dr. Lynn Maguire and Tina DeCruz in the Forest, studying how forest edges affect the herbaceous layer. It was a warm afternoon toward the end of the summer and the leaves had started to change colors and fall, and the forest floor was speckled with dots of sunlight falling through the canopy. It all formed a very impressionistic pattern. I was walking in the forest, eyes fixed on the ground, scanning for our indicator plants. We had resumed work after lunch, and with the warmth and Monet-like atmosphere pacifying my senses, my eyes blurred slightly, only responding to my targeted plants. Suddenly, right after a step forward, I felt the earth move. Coming from an area with frequent earthquakes (Taiwan), I knew it was not an earthquake. No, only a part of the earth moved, it only moved in one direction, and the part that moved felt slightly supple. I looked down and regained focus. It was a copperhead. I froze.

"The snake moved away, but as if to punish me for disturbing his nap, he slid pressed to my boot, full length. Through my boots, I could feel the cold skin and muscles moving. A minute or two after the event, I finally came to my senses, and whispered: 'Tina, I stepped on a copperhead.' Tina screamed for me."

– Chiru Chang, who graduated with a master's in 1992 and a doctorate in 1999, now in the Department of Landscape Architecture, Chinese Culture University.

Professor Ram Oren, second from right, reviews management prescriptions with a 2005 silviculture class. Duke Forest Photo Collection.

Water quality sampling in a tributary to New Hope Creek, about 1980. Duke Forest Photo Collection.

From Forestry to Earth and Environment

Although the Forestry School gradually expanded its curriculum beyond the study of southeastern forestry, Duke Forest continues to offer opportunities for broader environmental education. "Korstian's original plan for the Forestry School was to be the strongest in the South, and, understandably, early faculty and students gave primary emphasis to southern forestry issues," wrote Harold Steen in a 1989 article in *FOREM*. "However, academic scope gradually expanded to include the nation's forests and beyond."

A 1972 graduate of the Duke School of Forestry, current Forest resource manager Judson Edeburn has observed this expansion firsthand. He believes that the environmental movement sparked by the

The School of Forestry moved to a new Biological Sciences Building, shown here in the upper left, in 1962. Duke University Archives.

first Earth Day celebration in 1970 helped shift the direction of the Duke forestry school. "During the late 1960s the school followed a fairly traditional forestry curriculum, but in the early 1970s ecology professor Jim Wuenscher introduced a broader environmental management degree," recalls Edeburn. "This was the first nontraditional forestry degree and became a spark for future changes, because soon after that, in 1974, the school changed its name to Forestry and Environmental Studies."

In 1991, faculty from the School of Forestry and Environmental Studies joined with the Duke University Marine Laboratory under the umbrella of the School of the Environment. Then in 1995, the gift of $20 million from Peter M. Nicholas, a Boston business executive, precipitated the changing of the school's name to the Nicholas School of the Environment. In 2000, the school was renamed the Nicholas School of the Environment and Earth Sciences.

Faculty from throughout the Duke community appreciate the value of the Forest for their teaching

Ira Miller (MF 1940), Judson Edeburn (MF 1972), and William R. (Randy) Boggess (MF 1940) at Field Day 2006, celebrating the 75th anniversary of the Duke Forest. Photo by Roberta Reeves. Duke Forest Photo Collection.

and research. "The Forest is an excellent resource not only for the basis of the acreage but especially for the proximity," says William Stambaugh, professor emeritus of Forestry Pathology at Duke University. "Duke is blessed with a school forest right on its doorstep. There are many schools that have to travel hours and hours to get to their forest. Here you could be out on it or you could take your class out on it for an afternoon lab without any difficulty at all."

"The Forest really influences nearly all the teaching I do because it's easy to get to and easy for me to add a completely new dimension to teaching," says Daniel Richter, a professor at the School. "We have a network of soil pits in the Durham Division that we can use to look not only at the historical dimension

Duke Forest resource manager Judson Edeburn discusses a timber sale contract with Nicholas School students, 2004. Duke Forest Photo Collection.

Professor Dan Richter's graduate-level soil resources class in an Appling series soil derived from granitic gneiss, located in the Durham Division, September, 2005. This soil is an ancient, highly weathered upland soil, long used for agriculture. The area was an abandoned field when acquired by Duke and was subsequently planted with loblolly pine. Photo by Jason Jackson.

Teaching can involve hands-on experience, such as developing Global Positioning System (GPS) skills for mapping. Here, Nicholas School student Matt Andresen records a section of a walking trail requiring maintenance. Photo by Richard Broadwell. Duke Forest Photo Collection.

In 1996 the Nicholas School, along with the Duke Forest Office, moved to the Levine Science Research Center. The Office of the Duke Forest is currently in temporary space in the North Building, pending possible construction of new quarters for the Nicholas School.

of the soil but also see how nearby development is causing soil erosion. It's increasingly clear to more and more people that most universities have nothing like Duke Forest."

Norman Christensen feels that some of the Forest's educational potential remains untapped. "I think that the educational opportunities in Duke Forest are underused—they're inexhaustible," he says. "There's so much opportunity there not just in sciences but in other areas, such as the arts. It would be hard to imagine Duke University without Duke Chapel—and it would be hard to imagine it without Duke Forest. In many segments and many communities, the Forest is seen as emblematic of the university and the area."

Professor Norman L. Christensen Jr. has made extensive use of the Duke Forest for teaching and research. Duke Forest Photo Collection. Duke University Photography.

"While writing my thesis in 1967, I was hired by Fred White to be the superintendent of the Duke Forest. Fred was director and kept me from doing too much damage. There was a full time, three-man crew on the Forest. It included Robert Bell, a second man we called Pickle, and a third man I believe was named Jesse Hensen. Mr. Hensen worked for many years on the crew and, like Robert Bell, was still there when I left. Pickle retired in the summer of 1967 after many, many years on the crew. We had a retirement party at one of the picnic areas on the Forest for him, his family, and friends. One of the gifts was a brand new master key to all the Forest locks so he could drive to his favorite fishing spots for life. The key was safe with Pickle.

"One of our biggest jobs that year was to move the Forest equipment sheds. The original ones were located on the hill exactly where the chemistry building is now located, and when the University decide to build there, we had to move. There were spare parts of all kinds, lumber, a large antique grindstone, a small shop, and vehicle bays full of stuff. Outside there was a pile of culvert pipes and a large pile of cinders used for Forest road gravel. The cinders came from the old coal-fired steam plant just beyond the physics building. We moved everything to a new steel building near the Primate Center, where we set up a new shop and reorganized everything. It was a vast improvement over the old. During the move Robert Bell taught me a valuable lesson. When he saw me moving boxes around he said, 'You haven't moved much, have you? Here, do like this. Don't handle them more than once. If you pick it up, put it on the truck.'

"A second big project late in late winter/early spring of 1967 was planting the large fields on the recently acquired Dailey Farm in Alamance County with loblolly pines. We used our new farm tractor (with front-end loader) to pull the planting machine. It was a great new device.

"A sad event was the death of Dr. Clarence Korstian, the first dean of the School and the man who started it all. Fred White and I cleaned out his office; a place provided to him for his lifetime."

– William H. Sites, who received his master's of forestry in 1967 and a doctorate in 1972.

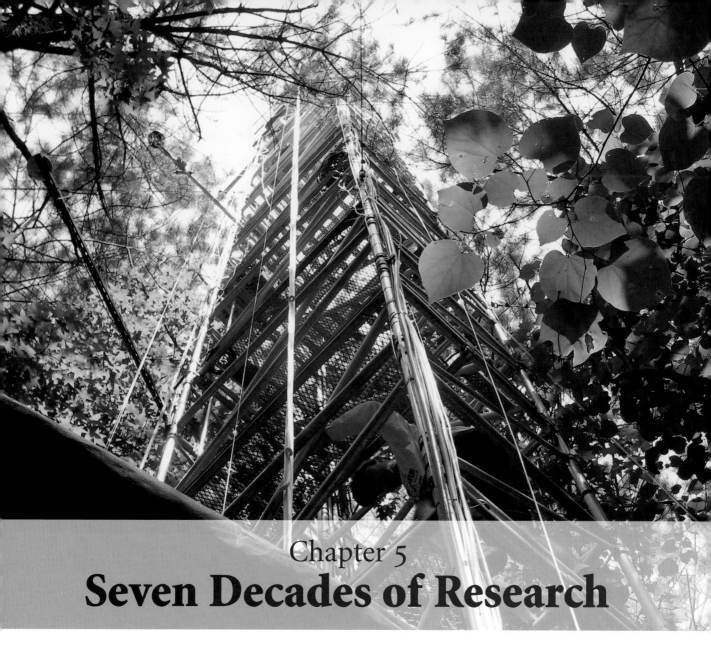

Chapter 5
Seven Decades of Research

O N A HUMID JULY MORNING I meet Michelle Hersh, a doctoral candidate in Duke's Biology Department, and David Bell, an incoming Nicholas School doctoral student, at a research site in Duke Forest's Eno Division off of the Stone Wall Fire Trail. After following summer fieldwork protocol (tuck pant legs into socks, apply insect repellent to deter chiggers, and stick duct tape on pants for potential tick removal), we walk into the cool darkness of a hardwood forest where a yellow-billed cuckoo calls from the canopy and a woodpecker chucks overhead.

Hersh and Bell are part of a team of researchers led by James S. Clark, a professor at the Nicholas School of the Environment and Earth Sciences and Biology Department at Duke University, and Paul Flikkema, an associate professor of electrical engineering at Northern Arizona University. Together they are developing a prototype wireless sensor network that is designed to gather data about the many environmental factors that maintain forest diversity.

Hersh shows me around the site, which contains an eight-foot-high deer exclosure and a number of laundry baskets strung from trees that are used to collect leaf litter. The heart of the wireless sensor site is a collection of towers (called nodes) arranged throughout the forest that house small gray boxes, called "WiSARDs" (an acronym for Wireless Sensing and Relay Device) that contain tiny computers. The nodes are wired to light sensors, temperature gauges, and soil moisture probes that collect short-term high-frequency data about the forest environment, including available light, temperature, and precipitation. The wizards are so precise they can detect a cloud moving overhead. Like a home computer network, the wizards send the data to a central node called the gateway. Although researchers continue to work out the kinks in this new technology, they hope that eventually the gateway will transmit the data to a principal location, like the laboratory. This would enable ecologists to have continuous ecological data from any habitat in which they set up a network.

Installation of deer exclusion fencing in the Clark Laboratory plots. Summer 2006. Duke Forest Photo Collection.

The wireless sensor network is just one of hundreds of research projects taking place on Duke Forest at any given time. In 2006 alone, different researchers were examining how urban development is affecting stream life and water quality, studying the mechanics behind hardwood tree seed dispersal, examining sprites (colorful lights emitted by lightning strikes), and monitoring plant and animal life in a forest bathed in elevated levels of carbon dioxide. Decaying stumps, ants, insects, birds, mammals, leaf litter—all these components of the Forest have been examined as scientists look for answers to pressing questions about the future of life on earth. Will trees grow faster in the future as the amount of carbon dioxide in the atmosphere continues to increase? And how will the changing climate affect other plant and animal life in forests?

Duke Forest has performed a unique service to the scientific community. Since 1931, the Forest has provided study sites for more than 475 master's projects, theses, and Ph.D. dissertations on a wide array of subjects, including forest management, silviculture, plant taxonomy, and invertebrate zoology. More than 450 published scientific papers have originated from research conducted on the property and currently more than $4 million annually in funded projects take place here. Universities and other institutions in the United States and worldwide have participated in this research, including Duke University, North Carolina State University, the University of North Carolina at Chapel Hill, the University of New Hampshire, and Griffith University in Australia; the U.S. Forest Service, the U.S. Environmental Protection Agency, the National Aeronautics and Space Administration, and the U.S. Department of Energy.

Researchers are attracted to the Forest for many reasons. The property offers a mosaic of habitat types for research, as well as great variation in soils, management history, topography, and forest stands. Researchers can capitalize on the Office of Duke Forest's 75-year-old archive of data, photographs, and maps. The Forest is just a short drive from the

Triangle's major research institutions. And scientists can be assured that the Forest will be available for ongoing research, whether their work encompasses a semester or a decade.

As the Piedmont landscape has changed over the past 75 years and the fields of forestry, biology, ecology, and environmental studies have advanced, the research in the Forest continues to build on previous work, creating "tributaries that feed into the broader river of knowledge," according to Richard Broadwell, former program director of the Forest. While early researchers such as Clarence Korstian examined basic forestry questions such as how specific silvicultural practices would affect timber quality, today's researchers are examining the pressing questions of the moment, such as monitoring how acid rain, ozone, and elevated levels of atmospheric carbon dioxide are affecting tree growth. "There is perhaps no other research and teaching forest in the world

quite like the Duke Forest, with its long-term and lasting impacts on several major scientific fields, and its long-standing continuity of use in forest and environmental education," says Daniel Richter.

Planting seedlings in the Open Top Chamber site, Durham Division, Compartment 70. Duke Forest Photo Collection.

Collecting data on "physical features." Durham Division, Compartment 16, 1936. Photo by C. F. Korstian. Duke Forest Photo Collection.

It Started with the Trees: The Permanent Sample Plots

Among the hundreds of research projects that have been based in the Forest, a few key studies demonstrate the magnitude of discoveries that have been made here. Ironically, the Forest's treasury of data was unearthed almost by accident some 30 years ago. When Norman Christensen began studying the ecology of southeastern forests by exploring the woodlands of Duke Forest in the mid-1970s he and Robert K. Peet, a botany professor at the University of North Carolina at Chapel Hill, made a curious discovery.

Permanent Sample plot 29, Korstian Division, Compartment 2, after thinning, 1940. Photo by J. R. Jester. Duke Forest Photo Archives.

"As we walked in the Forest, we saw all these trees with numbers painted on them," says Christensen. "But the numbers were beginning to fade, and we had no idea what they signified. In the mid-1970s, Ben Jayne, the dean of the Forestry School, was cleaning out some filing cabinets and discovered some of Clarence Korstian's records, as well as some old hand-tinted glass lantern slides with scenes from the Forest. We studied them and realized that they contained the data about the numbered plots in the forests, called the "permanent sample plots." Suddenly we knew what everything was. It was like finding the Rosetta Stone!"

Between 1933 and 1947, Korstian and soil scientist Theodore Coile had established a set of 87 study plots in the Forest (now known as the "permanent sample plots" or "PSPs") that ranged in size from one-tenth to one acre and encompassed various ages and forest habitat types. The team identified the tree species in each plot, numbered the trees, and then measured and recorded the height, diameter, and crown length of every tree within the plots.

Korstian established the plots in part because of recommendations from state forester W. W. Ashe. "When you look at Korstian's first activities on the Forest, you can see that he followed Ashe's report almost to the letter," says Christensen. In the 1926 report "Suggestions concerning the Forest Lands" that Ashe wrote for Duke University, he advised that "the large number of species, the wide range in age-classes, and the condition of growth afford an excellent opportunity for experimental work with small unit plots, which could advantageously be used as adjuncts to classroom courses in silviculture."

When Korstian arrived at Duke he realized that the Forest provided a microcosm of a landscape that was being radically transformed by the rapid abandonment of agriculture that began in the 1920s. "Loblolly pine forests like those found in Duke Forest today didn't become common until after 1900," explains Christensen. "Before that most of this region contained abandoned farm land and extensive

Many of the photographs used in this book have come from an extensive collection of black and white photos taken over the years by Dr. Korstian and his associates. The photos are carefully documented in typed jackets which contain several prints and a negative. The photos have been scanned under the direction of Richard Broadwell, former Program Director on the Forest.

Many of the photos have an accompanying 3" by 4" glass lantern slide, reportedly hand tinted by Mrs. Korstian. Former Forestry and Environmental Studies Dean, Benjamin Jayne, became interested in this collection and had a number of these slides reproduced as color prints in the late 1970s. These prints are on display in the Office of the Duke Forest.

Permanent Sample Plot 23 was established in the Durham Division in the early 1930s. The historical information collected from such areas has become an important source of ecological data. Professor William Maughan is pictured in the foreground. Duke Forest Photo Collection.

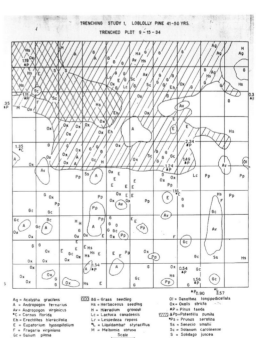

Detailed map of the Trench Plot Study, 1934. Office of the Duke Forest.

mature pine stands were uncommon. When the fields began regrowing in pines, people didn't know how to manage them to get maximum productivity. Korstian established the PSPs around a set of experiments that focused on answering basic questions about the management of loblolly pines or hardwoods, such as what happens when I thin the forest, or prune the trees, or vary the number of trees I plant per acre."

Korstian's attention to detail made his records all the more valuable for future researchers. "Korstian was incredibly meticulous," marvels Christensen. "He kept records on everything with great care, which means that we can go back to the same trees that he surveyed in 1931 and examine them today. The PSPs are a remarkable data set on the Forest. There are relatively few places in the world where you have that kind of long-term information."

Early measurements taken in a permanent sample plot. Duke Forest Photo Collection.

The discovery of the PSP records proved to be a watershed moment for Christensen and Peet, who had teamed up to examine fundamental questions of forest ecology, using Duke Forest as their model. The PSPs provided them with a sort of ecological hindsight about the history of the Forest. With funding from the National Science Foundation, the team established 230 permanent plots and analyzed the woody plant and herb communities within each plot. "Our

Professor Herb Bormann walks with Dan Richter, professor of soils and ecology, and Dr. Rob MacDonald, an ecology Ph.D. graduate, during early spring 2003 through the upland oak-hickory stand known as the Bormann Plot, in the Durham Division of Duke Forest. Bormann was impressed by the continuity and the change in the vegetation since the time he was a graduate student in forest ecology at Duke in the early 1950s. After Duke, Bormann went on to become a world-renowned ecosystem ecologist; he taught at Dartmouth College and Yale University for many years and was a cofounder and principal investigator for many of the primary experiments at the Hubbard Brook Experimental Forest in the White Mountains of New Hampshire. Richter and MacDonald had invited Bormann to Duke to give a seminar to the University Program in Ecology and to revisit the Duke Forest. In Bormann's seminar, not only did he review the early history of Duke's ecology and forestry programs, he also recounted how his graduate education had led directly to his conceptual ideas about forest watersheds as ecosystems and to the initiation of the Hubbard Brook watershed studies. Bormann attributed his ideas about using gaged watersheds to study biogeochemistry and nutrient cycling to a visit he made to Coweeta Hydrologic Laboratory in western North Carolina, a field trip in a soils class with Professor Ted Coile of Duke's School of Forestry.

research focused on using principles of forest biology to look at forest change, such as rates of reproduction and mortality in trees," explains Christensen. "We were trying to do for trees what insurance companies do for people—develop predictions about mortality. The PSPs turned out to be extraordinarily useful in helping us develop patterns of tree death and die-off."

In 1987, Christensen and Peet published a paper titled "Competition and Tree Death" in the journal *BioScience* that synthesized their research from Duke Forest. They concluded that after trees become established in a forest, certain trees will die, so that the forest essentially naturally thins itself. The surviving trees form the core of the so-called climax forest. Their findings became a law about self-thinning that applies to forests all over the world.

Korstian's Peers

When Korstian and his colleagues began working at Duke Forest, some of the abandoned agricultural land looked like a war zone, as photos from the time show areas in the Forest where three-foot-deep erosion gullies gashed the bare soil and the entire layer of topsoil had washed away. Daniel Richter is fond of quoting University of North Carolina professor C. S. Johnston, who described the southern landscape in the 1930s as "a miserable panorama of unpainted shacks, rain-gullied fields, straggling fences, rattle-trap Fords, dirt, poverty, disease, drudgery, and monotony that stretches for a thousand miles across the cotton belt." But Korstian and his colleagues had an utterly different reaction to the scenery.

"**W**e've been conducting various surveys of microbial diversity in Duke Forest for 20 years, with emphasis on mushroom-forming fungi but also including other fungi, eukaryotes, and bacteria. Fungi are some of the most abundant and diverse groups of forest microorganisms. Most of our research involves basic taxonomic collecting for systematics research, as well as general collecting to document species diversity.

"The Duke Herbarium contains over 5,000 fungal specimens, nearly half of which were collected in the Forest. From 2000 to 2004 we employed a "microbial observatory" approach to perform a combined survey of above- and below-ground diversity of fungi from the Forest. Using DNA sequences as our sampling unit, we conducted a large-scale survey of fungi within permanent sample plots used by earlier Duke ecologists to study plant communities across the Forest.

Hygrocybe sp., *one of over 5,000 fungal specimens for which DNA sequences have been collected. Duke Forest Photo Collection.*

"The Duke Forest Mycological Observatory (DFMO) database contains more than 5,000 annotated DNA sequences collected from different habitats in Duke Forest, including data from individual specimens as well as clone-libraries of total DNA from soil and litter. Every sequence is identified to at least an approximate taxonomic group, and every record is GIS-referenced. The development of our DFMO project was directed largely by the needs of ecological researchers working on various projects in Duke Forest, including the FACE [Free-Air CO_2 Enrichment] research site and other Piedmont forest sites."

– Dr. Rytas Vilgalys, Biology Department, Duke University, July 2006

"Ecologists and foresters . . . quickly became fascinated with how plant vegetation responded to this landscape being abandoned by farmers," write Daniel Richter and Daniel Markewitz in their book *Understanding Soil Change*. "In fact, the entire concept of plant succession was greatly enriched by classical studies of old fields in the central Carolina Piedmont by Billings (1938), Coile (1940), and Oosting (1942)." W. D. Billings, Theodore Coile, and Henry J. Oosting were among the first faculty members of the Duke School of Forestry and the Department of Botany to study the forest ecology of Duke Forest. Each of them contributed greatly to the fledgling field of silviculture. "These pioneer Duke Forest ecologists immediately understood that they were studying a landscape undergoing enormous change, and they had the wisdom to understand that change as an exemplar for forest change in general," says Christensen. "They also understood that these changes occurred on time scales that would far exceed their lifetimes and they recognized that, if benchmarked and recorded carefully, their data would be priceless to generations of ecologists who would study these same landscapes. They constructed a framework for understanding both the pattern and mechanisms of successional change."

A leader in the burgeoning field of soil science, Theodore Coile analyzed how soil properties influence tree growth. By looking at the correlation between the height of trees at a certain age, and the type of soil in which it grew, Coile developed a set of "site index curves," essentially a graph predicting tree growth. "Coile was farsighted in terms of seeing this degraded landscape as being economically valuable as it transitioned into trees," Richter remarks. "His concept of using a soil profile to predict how a tree will grow over 50 years has proven to be amazingly useful over time. He developed these growth prediction models for four or five pine species. If you look at how trees are planted and grown throughout the world you can use the same pathway to predict tree growth. In a generic way he was one of the first to put together a formula about how to grow trees."

The regenerative power of Piedmont woodlands was also the catalyst for botanist Henry J. Oosting to refine the concept of plant succession. Using Duke Forest as a model, Oosting published "An Ecological Analysis of the Plant Communities of Piedmont, North Carolina" in *American Midland Naturalist* in 1942. Oosting's paper provides an exhaustive description of all the major plant communities within the Forest ranging from

A Duke Forest crew using a Lauther's planting machine drawn by a TD-6 tractor, 1952. This plowed field was used for agriculture during 1951. One-year-old loblolly pine seedlings are being used for planting stock, with a 7 x 7 spacing. Photo by K. L. Carvell. Duke Forest Photo Collection.

successional communities such as abandoned fields to more stable communities like stream bluffs. Written in an approachable style, Oosting's paper provides an illustration of the Forest's habitats that he said could apply generally "to a large part of the lower Piedmont Plateau, probably from Alabama to Virginia," and was "particularly applicable to most of the Piedmont area of North Carolina." Oosting described in detail the changing array of plant species that invaded old fields and concluded that "succession following abandonment of upland fields is represented by distinct communities which follow each other rapidly in the early stages." His analysis of Piedmont plant communities remains the basic reference on secondary forest succession in this region.

Five years after the publication of this paper, one of Oosting's graduate students, Katherine Keever, initiated research that branched from Oosting's findings. "In the autumn of 1947 . . . I began working on the causes of old-field succession in North Carolina,"

Keever recalls in "A Retrospective View of Old-Field Succession after 35 years," published in *American Midland Naturalist* in October 1983.

> The sequence of species invading and dominating abandoned farmland in North Carolina had been determined by Crafton and Wells (1934) and Oosting (1942) with little disagreement. . . . Dr. Oosting admitted (personal communication) that although he knew the sequence of species in early old-field succession, he did not know what caused these distinct and fast changes and challenged me to find the causes.

Working in the old fields of Duke Forest, Keever concluded that the types of species that dominate the various stages of regrowth are determined by plants' basic characteristics, such as seed germination. Keever's findings are still widely regarded. "Keever's work was not fully appreciated at the time," says Christensen. "But it made clear that much of the pattern of change in succession following old-field abandonment was a consequence of differences in species' life history traits such as patterns of establishment and growth and survival."

These first major ecological inquiries centered on Duke Forest became a road map for future generations of scientists. "The work of Korstian, Billings,

Trenching for the Short Leaf Pine Site Index Study, Durham Division, Compartment 15, 1933. Photo by C. F. Korstian. Duke Forest Photo Collection.

Durham Division, Couch Tract, 1950. Succession. A cultivated field abandoned 5 years previously, with loblolly pine now dominating the broomsedge. Photo by B. F. Smith. Duke Forest Photo Collection.

Oosting, Coile, and Keever created a framework upon which others could hang much more detailed questions," says Christensen. "They not only described the general pattern of change, but they provided key understanding to the mechanisms of that change. Korstian, for example, established clearly the importance of competition from trees in determining the composition of forest communities. Oosting and Billings (along with Paul Kramer) put this process on a physiological basis by documenting the importance of species requirements for light and water in determining when they appeared in succession. With this foundation, people like Bob Peet and me could ask questions about how this process varied from one place to another or from one time to another.

The high deer population is affecting the ecology of the Forest. Duke Forest Photo Collection.

We could also use their data, revisit their study areas, and ask questions about how much forest change was a consequence of succession following disturbance, and how much of it was and is related to ongoing changes that are independent of agricultural abandonment, such as variations in climate, changes in landscape pattern, invasive exotic species like Japanese bamboo grass and 'explosive' native species like white-tailed deer."

Today's Research

Research in the Forest changes over time, in keeping with trends in environmental science research generally. In the 1970s and 1980s, the Forest housed the Southeast's primary study site for the National Acid Precipitation Assessment Program (NAPAP). The project examined "the alleged 15–25% decline in growth of pine forests in the Piedmont of the Carolinas during the past decade," according to a 1988 report by the Duke University Academic Subcommittee of the Land Resources Committee. "Such declines have been recently documented for central Europe and certain forests in New England, and are thought to be the result of acid precipitation in those areas." Currently, scientists are grappling with the hot topic of climate change.

Climate Change Research in the Forest

Even while discussing the dire topic of climate change, Jeffrey S. Pippen's cheerful demeanor erases any thoughts of the proverbial "gloom and doom scientist." A research associate at the Nicholas School, Pippen spent a spring morning in 2006 showing me around the FACE (Free-Air CO_2 Enrichment) site in Duke Forest's Blackwood Division. The most highly funded research project that has ever taken place in the Forest, the FACE site houses multiple studies that are examining how elevated levels of carbon dioxide (CO_2) in the atmosphere of the future will affect different components of a forested ecosystem.

Although people sometimes describe the FACE site as a global warming study, Pippen says that is an inaccurate label. "When the project began in 1996 and we started giving tours of the site, 'global warming' was a controversial buzz phrase," he says. "In fact, we aren't studying global warming at all.

Open Top Chamber site, Durham Division, Compartment 70, 1992. Duke Forest Photo Collection.

Studying Sprites

In a trailer in an open field in the Blackwood Division, a team led by Steven Cummer, assistant professor in the Electrical and Computer Engineering Department at Duke University, monitors radio emissions produced by lightning. The trailer houses computers that record data from two pairs of magnetic field sensors buried in the field. "With our Duke Forest–deployed sensors, we record the radio emissions from just about any lightning stroke in the United States and just about any strong lightning stroke in North and Central America," explains Cummer. "We use the data in several ways, including simply studying lightning over a very large geographic region. Most previous measurements have not sampled such a large region and we are finding that there are more lightning strokes with unusual characteristics, such as very big charge transfers, than was previously appreciated. And we use the data to study some of the more unusual effects lightning produces, such as sprites and terrestrial gamma ray flashes.

"Duke Forest is ideal for our project for several reason. The biggest advantage to working here is that we are removed from strong sources of noise such as powerlines, cars, and motors. So we are in a remote place, but we also have the infrastructure we need to shelter and power the system. And the great support that the Office of the Duke Forest provides has been incredibly helpful."

We're studying how rising atmospheric carbon dioxide, which is part of global climate change, affects the growth of a pine forest ecosystem."

Gases in the atmosphere such as carbon dioxide and water vapor are often called greenhouse gases because they trap energy from the sun and warm the earth. Most scientists agree that increased emissions of carbon dioxide and other greenhouse gases are trapping more heat in the earth's atmosphere, thus causing the earth's temperature to rise. People produce CO_2 emissions through various means, including industry, operating vehicles, burning fossil fuels (the source of most of our electricity), and deforestation.

Scientists have determined historic levels of atmospheric CO_2 by dating and analyzing air bubbles trapped in ice cores from Antarctica. It appears that CO_2 levels began to increase when people started burning fossil fuels after the advent of the industrial revolution and the development of gasoline engines. Scientists believe that by the year 2050, atmospheric CO_2 will have increased 1.5 times over today's level. Not only will the planet be warmer (some projections suggest that the earth could become 2.5 to 10.4 degrees hotter by 2100), but extreme weather events

Aerial view of the Free-Air CO_2 Enrichment (FACE) site, Blackwood Division. Photo by Will Owens. Duke Forest Photo Collection.

Free-Air CO$_2$ Enrichment (FACE) rings in the Blackwood Division. Blackwood Mountain is visible in the distance. Duke University Photography.

such as hurricanes are likely to increase and melting glaciers could cause sea levels to rise and inundate low-lying coastal areas. According to the Environmental Protection Agency's Global Warming Web site, "the 20th century's 10 warmest years all occurred in the last 15 years of the century."

Such alarming projections are the catalyst for much of the current research in the Forest. "Climate change is one of the most important and unpredictable challenges facing environmental scientists," says James Clark. "It will occur at scales that are difficult to study."

The FACE site is almost like a time warp that replicates a forest of the future. Before the development of FACE technology, climate change projects typically occurred in artificial environments such as greenhouses or phytotrons (specialized growth chambers). Developed by scientists at the Brookhaven National Laboratory, FACE technology is a completely "chamber-free" experiment that enables scientists to study the impacts of elevated CO$_2$ on an ecosystem in the open air, subject to all the vagaries of weather and seasonal changes.

The Duke Forest FACE site contains eight circular plots that each measure 100 feet in diameter. In seven of the plots, 32 vent pipes rise 80 feet from the ground, extending over the loblolly canopy and bathing the forested area within the rings in a constant stream of CO_2. The CO_2 emissions match the level of CO_2 projected to be in the earth's atmosphere in the year 2050 (560 parts per million). Each plot is paired with and compared to a control plot that is not exposed to excess CO_2.

There are other FACE sites around the world in different ecosystems, including the Mojave Desert in Arizona, a tropical savanna in Australia, and a grassland in Switzerland. When scientists from Brookhaven were searching for a Southeastern forest in which to establish a site, Duke Forest became a suitable candidate for several reasons. "For one thing, we needed a flat site with an even canopy of trees that was relatively uniform, which we found in this even-aged loblolly stand," explains William Schlesinger, dean of the Nicholas School and one of the lead scientists at the Duke FACE site. "At the time there had been a lot of talk about carbon sequestration in the United States, which is the idea that forests could act as carbon sinks and store excess atmospheric CO_2 in the future. Many people thought that the Southeast might be a good candidate for sequestration because of the dense forest cover. Professor Boyd Strain, who taught in Duke's Botany Department, had done a lot of greenhouse work here where he'd shown that loblolly was very responsive to CO_2. So it seemed a good idea to test the carbon sink theory in a site in the Southeast, because if we didn't have a sink here, then that would close the argument on whether forests could provide sinks. And, there was also the connection to Duke University and the high quality of the ecology and botany programs and the Nicholas School." Duke faculty and students currently participate in roughly two-thirds of the projects at the FACE site, and researchers from other institutions such as West Virginia University, the University of Illinois, and the University of New Hampshire work on the remainder.

The air under the 23-year-old loblolly stand that houses the FACE site is filled with a loud humming noise. Pippen explains that it's the sound of the fan units that blow the ambient and CO_2-enriched air into the plots. Every day, a truck delivers liquid CO_2 from a Virginia fertilizer plant to special holding

Emeritus professor Boyd Strain. Duke University Archives.

tanks at the site, currently at a cost of about $1 million a year. The CO_2 is converted to gas in a passive heat exchanger and then funneled through copper pipes to each CO_2-enriched plot. When we walk on a boardwalk into the dense pine stand in one of the plots I see a seemingly chaotic jumble of research tools covering the thick carpet of brown pine needles: laundry baskets, wires, rain gauges, PVC pipes, coolers, ropes,

Research associate Jeffrey S. Pippen collecting data at the Free-Air CO_2 Enrichment (FACE) site. Photo by Ida Phillips Lynch.

and tiny brightly colored flags. Pippen explains that the boardwalk divides the research area into quadrants and each research group marks its turf with the color-coded flagging.

With Pippen's help I begin to decipher the meaning of all this apparent clutter. In general, all of these tools are used to assess the growth of every component of the loblolly pine forest such as trees, shrubs, roots, and insects, and compare it to the same organisms in the control grids. The laundry baskets collect leaf litter (anything that falls from a tree, including sticks, leaves, berries, insects, and pine needles) that researchers analyze in the laboratory. Spring-loaded steel bands with precision scales that measure tree growth to 1/100th of an inch hug every pine tree. Wires snaking into the ground are connected to probes that monitor soil moisture and temperature, and cameras that photograph subterranean processes such as the growth of fungus on tree roots.

Scientists from the National Center for Atmospheric Research on the Chemical Emission, Loss, Transformation and Interaction within Canopies (CELTIC) project in the Blackwood Division. Photo by Judson Edeburn. Duke Forest Photo Collection.

In a trailer at the entrance to the site, two site managers from the Brookhaven National Laboratory spend their days operating several computer stations, where they keep a vigilant eye on the entire project, watching charts and graphs to ensure that the CO_2 is being released at the right level and monitoring the instruments that track the wind speed and direction at the towers.

Findings to Date

Although research at the FACE site is ongoing, the scientists working here have published many papers in the first decade of study. "There is little question that the rise of CO_2 is altering plant photosynthesis," says Dan Richter, who has studied the impacts of elevated CO_2 on soil in the FACE site. "We also think that rising CO_2 is directly affecting soil," he explains. "Soil doesn't change overnight but through decades of time. So we are really interested in how increased CO_2 will affect the weathering of rock, because CO_2 is corrosive and breaks down rock in the process of soil formation. We began working at FACE with the hypothesis that weathering is accelerated. We started looking at this out in the FACE site and then continued in the lab and I think we've convincingly demonstrated that weathering can be accelerated." Although some people may not be overly concerned with what is going on underfoot, Richter explains that accelerated weathering affects the availability of nutrients in the soil and "will matter to future generations in terms of how they understand the global carbon cycle and manage elevated CO_2 levels."

The accelerated photosynthesis is having a more immediate effect on plant life in the FACE site. Schlesinger and his colleagues published a paper in *Ecological Studies* in 2006 that concluded that "photosynthetic rates by canopy foliage have increased up to 50% over controls." As expected, the accelerated photosynthesis results in faster tree growth: In eight years the loblolly pines in the experimental plots grew 13 to 27 percent faster than those in the control rings. More years of study are needed, however, to determine just how the elevated CO_2 affects tree growth at the FACE site, since soil nutrient levels and moisture availability change over time.

Another recent study has attracted an enormous amount of media attention, as is often the case, because of its link to human health. A team led by Jacqueline Mohan, whose Ph.D. research focused on plant growth at the Duke FACE site, found that vine growth has exploded in the elevated CO_2 rings. Over the course of five years, poison ivy (*Toxicodendron radicans*) in the CO_2-enriched rings grew 149 percent faster than plants in the control plots. "With any kind of vertical plant like a tree or a sunflower, for example, much of the growth response goes into the structure that holds it up, which essentially consumes the products of photosynthesis," explains Schlesinger. "But since vines lean on other plants, they don't need to invest in their structure, so all their photosynthesis goes into producing more leaves."

As well, the poison ivy in the enriched plots produced more urushiol, the chemical irritant in the plant that causes an allergic reaction in approximately 80 percent of the population. "Our findings indicated that under future levels of atmospheric CO_2, *T. radicans* may grow larger and become more noxious than it is today," the team wrote in a paper published in *PNAS* (*Proceedings of the National Academy of Sciences*) on June 13, 2006.

> Given the global distribution of this and other closely related species, these results have implications for forest dynamics and human health. Increased abundance of woody vines in old-growth and fragmented forests is reducing tree regeneration and increasing tree mortality in tropical and temperate regions. . . . If *Toxicodendron* becomes both more abundant and more irritating to sensitive individuals, which include ~ 80% of the human population, it is likely that this plant will become a greater health problem in the future.

Not surprisingly, when the study was published, the news made headlines across the country, including *The New York Times*.

Research and the Future

Back in the shady forest in the Eno Division, climate change seems very real. "Everybody talks about the weather but nobody does anything about it," quipped Mark Twain, but here at the Duke Forest scientists such as James Clark are racing to develop technology that might help us "do something" about climate change, by helping future landowners and land managers understand how natural habitats will react to changing environmental conditions—such as the increasingly arid conditions projected for the Southeast in the future.

"The diversity of forests depends on weather," explains Clark. "The amount of moisture available for trees and the temperatures at which they grow determine survival and reproduction. Different species react to variation in weather differently, with some species better able to withstand drought and others tolerating extreme low temperatures in winter. Typically, ecologists studying diversity have information on climate, that is, 'average weather,' but not on the weather variables that actually control growth, reproduction, and survival. The wireless sensor network allows us to obtain information on

At left is a scaffolding type tower supporting instrumentation in an open field. At right is a Remote Automated Weather Station (RAWS) maintained by the North Carolina Division of Forest Resources for collecting fire weather data. The data can also be accessed by researchers using the Duke Forest. Duke Forest Photo Collection.

soil moisture, temperature, light availability, and transpiration rates. Together with observations on the trees themselves, these data will allow us to determine how different species are likely to respond to increasing aridity in the Southeast."

Clark sees practical applications for the research: "The information we collect in the field will help us develop models of forest development over time, particularly in the context of climate change scenarios. These models will help us anticipate change in biodiversity, identify species that may be in trouble, and suggest mitigation strategies."

Researchers such as Michelle Hersh and Clark see many advantages to conducting research in Duke Forest, including the freedom provided by working in a natural environment. "Duke Forest allows us to conduct large scale experiments on elevated CO_2, tornadoes and hurricanes, fires, and deer exclusion," says Clark. "The experiments help us identify the interacting variables with climate change."

There are practical advantages as well. Hersh's doctorate study is about the effects of fungal pathogens on tree seedlings, so the proximity of the Forest to her lab at the Duke Biology Department is vital for collecting weekly seedling samples and culturing pathogenic fungi before they become too degraded to grow in the lab. "The fact that it's here is priceless, in the sense that we can be at our field sites in 15 minutes," says Schlesinger. "That's spectacular, not just for researchers, but also because you can take a class there in 15 minutes and show them projects in real time and place."

Hersh also appreciates the Forest's straightforward permitting process for researchers. "And the staff has been wonderful in providing information about feasible study sites in the forest, and helping us with maintenance problems and issues, such as constructing our deer exclosures and removing fallen trees from access roads," she adds.

Although difficult to measure, the Forest also offers researchers the type of insights into the environment that can only be gleaned from nature. "When you get out in the field you can see natural changes unfolding before your eyes," says Dave Bell. "You see things happening and it raises questions, like why are these vines growing here? No matter

Professor Emily Bernhardt evaluates the ability of forests to improve water quality: "Understanding the role stream ecosystems play in watershed nutrient retention is a critical frontier in biogeochemistry. A growing body of research demonstrates the important effect stream ecosystems have in altering the form, timing, and magnitude of watershed nitrogen losses." Duke Forest Photo Collection.

Research associate Peter Harrell positions a reflector for a radar imaging study funded by the National Aeronautics and Space Administration (NASA) in the early 1990s. Duke University Photography.

how much you can automate your research, it's still invaluable to be able to spend time in a natural environment like Duke Forest."

What will future researchers study in the Forest? As CO_2 levels continue to rise, then the Forest of the future will likely endure more hurricanes, changes in tree composition, and possibly the loss of species that reach the southern end of their ranges in North Carolina's Piedmont that will be forced to move farther north as their range shifts. As in the past, the changing landscape of the Forest and the Piedmont will guide the direction of future research. "There are several different dimensions to Duke Forest's value as a research site, but the one that strikes me as being so important is the scholarly value of the forest," says Christensen. "The more it is studied the more valuable it becomes. It's the ecological equivalent of a rare book room—it contains an accumulation of history and potential for future research. Just as Korstian didn't realize the value of what he began, we don't know what kind of research people will conduct there in the future."

Graduate students Kim Novick and Jehn-Yi Juang erect tri-sonic anemometers for wind profile study. Duke Forest Photo Collection.

Chapter 6
Managing the Forest and Its Resources

I N 75 YEARS, THE DAY-TO-DAY MANAGEMENT of Duke Forest has changed dramatically with advances in technology, forestry, and research. Whereas early forest managers relied on maps and ledgers to record the locations and types of timber stands, today's forest managers rely on GPS units and spreadsheets. At the same time, many of the skills required to manage this research forest are the same as they were during Clarence Korstian's tenure from 1931 to 1958.

Like his predecessors, Judson (Judd) Edeburn, Duke Forest resource manager, possesses the diverse set of skills required of someone who must fill the roles of forester, researcher, educator, and caretaker. People skills are essential for a position that requires interaction with a wide array of people including the general public, researchers, Duke University officials, and contract workers. Edeburn may never have what you could call a typical day at work. His schedule can be disrupted at any moment by an urgent call from a logger who felled a tree across a power line, causing a fire, or a hiker who wandered off a trail and became disoriented and lost his way.

Judson Edeburn became the Duke Forest resource manager in 1978. Duke Forest Photo Collection.

And then there are more unusual phone calls, such as the fellow who called about the squirrel problem. An irate Duke Forest neighbor complained that the Forest staff was obviously not feeding their squirrels enough because they were invading his property and devouring his bird seed. Edeburn advised the caller that gray squirrels are wild animals and the Forest staff cannot control their movements. Although the Forest offers an abundance of native food, this savvy squirrel obviously preferred bird food.

Edeburn's comfort level in the deep woods is obvious if you walk with him in the Forest on a muggy, sticky summer day. Without a skip in his step, he will charge through a dense briar thicket or tangle of vines. As he drives or walks around the Forest, checking on a logging operation, or escorting a reporter from a local paper for a story, Edeburn stays tuned to anything amiss in the Forest, noting a muddy pothole that needs more gravel, a guy-wire that's popped out of one of the research towers, or a carpet of *Microstegium* that's choking the roadside.

A 1972 master of forestry graduate from Duke, Edeburn started working at Duke Forest in 1978. Early in his career he spent about half his time in the field. Like most people who are attracted to a field like forestry, he prefers outdoor activities to computer time, but today he probably spends more than three-fourths of his time in the office, dealing with the administrative issues that come with managing 7,046 acres, four staff members, several student assistants, and who knows how many ravenous squirrels.

A History of Management at Duke Forest

Much of what is known about the history of the management of the Forest has been gleaned from conversations with former directors, superintendents, contractors, and others who have worked in the Forest over the past 75 years. Edeburn has sorted through hundreds of files to piece together the development of the Forest's research projects, management issues, and financial history. The so-called Brain Book, a large black volume that chronicles the development of the permanent sample plots (PSPs) plantation records, together with research files and Korstian's reports, provide much of the link to the past. Numerous old maps and a voluminous slide and photo archive contribute invaluable visual information to the story.

The basic tenets of the management goals for the Forest are the same today as they were in 1931. In the

1931 *Forestry Bulletin*, Korstian outlined three objectives for the Forest: that it was to be used as an outdoor laboratory for research, as a place where students could study, and as a demonstration forest—and, in general, that is how the Forest is managed today. The greatest change is the breadth and diversity of the teaching and research, which used to be more focused on tree growth and understanding relationships between soil and trees than it is now.

"Today the research has expanded into areas such as global climate change, aquatic systems, and microclimates," says Edeburn. "But it is still connected to the past. For example, monitoring the tree growth in the FACE [Free-Air CO_2 Enrichment] site evolved from the study of the relationships between soil and trees, and now researchers are looking at the relationships between the atmosphere, soil, and the growth of trees and other plants."

Researchers in the Forest are still examining how plant communities respond to the environment, whether they're studying soil fertility or productivity or changes in the atmosphere. Even in the long-term plots, people are studying changes in plant communities over time and the communities' response to the physical environment. "They're studying how those sites have been managed and changed over time, for example, whether it was originally an old field or uneven-aged hardwoods—is it still supporting that 50 years later?" Edeburn notes that "many of the PSPs that Dr. Korstian established are still in existence and have been used by Norm Christensen, Bob Peet, and others. The data taken on these plots over the years is irreplaceable."

The Forest staff strives to manage the Forest in part to be responsive to various teaching and research projects by maintaining a mosaic of natural communities in the Forest, and a good age class distribution among tree stands. Sometimes researchers make specific management requests for a project, such as a request for a large area of even-aged forest, which the Office accommodated by harvesting a 60-acre area in the Dailey Division. Many research

Students in a fire ecology class assisting in a prescribed burn. Duke Forest Photo Collection.

Students Matt Brinkman and Ryne Conley from Virginia Tech sample sweetgum, yellow poplar, and red maple for the Sustainable Engineered Materials Institute (SEMI). Durham Division, Compartment 71. Photo by Judson Edeburn. Duke Forest Photo Collection.

projects require replicated plots that can only be created in a large physical area of a given habitat type, so now the staff is trying to increase the average size of forested stands so that multiple plots can be established in a homogeneous area.

Often management activities in early research sites serendipitously provide a perfect setup for a later project. "In the early 1980s, Ken Knoerr, a professor of environmental meteorology at Duke University, needed a research site with a smooth canopy, so that spurred us to harvest about 90 acres in the Blackwood Division and replant it with loblolly pines," recalls Edeburn. "If we had not done the harvesting and planting back in 1981, we would not have had a site that was suitable for the FACE project."

An advisory committee reviews any projects that are going to be of such a size and duration that they will require a substantial commitment of resources. The committee also reviews initiatives from outside the University that might affect the Forest and provides input to the University administration for further action.

Demonstration of sustainable forest management practices remains an integral part of the Duke Forest's mission. Korstian Division, Compartment 32. Duke Forest Photo Collection.

2006 Nicholas School graduate Katherine Armstrong examines a recently completed precommercial thinning project. Duke Forest Photo Collection.

Commercial thinning operation, Blackwood Division, Compartment 8, 2006. Duke Forest Photo Collection.

Duke Forest as a Unique Resource

Duke Forest has always provided researchers and educators with a unique set of characteristics that are not found in many research forests. "One theme among forest managers seems to be that that the closer a research forest is to the campus the more it will be used," says Edeburn. "If a research site is difficult to get to, it can diminish the value of the site. Some forests are far enough away from the institution that they have facilities there like cabins or dorms or office space, and of course we don't need that because we're so close to campus. Assisting faculty and students in their use of the Forest is one of our office's most important objectives. We try to do whatever it takes to answer their questions and provide support for their projects, no matter how large or small."

The Office also boasts a vast archive of data, records, maps, photographs, and other materials. These extensive records are of great use to researchers, as they can reveal how different sites in the Forest have been managed over time. With the expertise of former program director, Richard Broadwell, and student assistants, the Office has entered more of this data into GIS (Geographic Information System), so it is easier for researchers to query when they are looking for a specific type of site, such as pine plantations, that are on different soils. "Just as one example," notes Edeburn, "researcher Kim Ludovichi was interested in the decomposition of stumps, so we found varying ages of stumps by pointing her in the direction of different aged forest stands."

Revenue Production in the Forest

Balancing the needs of the Forest itself and its numerous research projects is a continuing concern for the Office of the Duke Forest. As in Korstian's tenure, timber revenue still provides the bulk of the Forest's operational budget. "Timber sales from our annual harvests currently provide about 80 percent

This longleaf pine plantation was established in 1935. It has been periodically thinned and now is prescribed burned at two- to three-year intervals. Durham Division, Compartment 72. Duke Forest Photo Collection.

of the operating budget for Duke Forest," says Edeburn. "Every year we regenerate 40 to 50 acres of forest. We may harvest in response to specific research opportunities, but we also harvest to provide a mosaic of diverse habitats, promote healthy timber stands, and provide demonstration areas for class exercises. Based on the growth rate of timber stands in the forest we know how much of the forest we can sustainably harvest. We apply a set of constraints to that on an acreage basis, because we don't harvest in established research sites, Natural Heritage areas, streamside buffers, or aesthetic buffers. We're on a 10-year harvest planning cycle and much of the harvesting takes place in natural or planted pine stands."

The Forest staff's harvesting activities occasionally prompt questions from Forest visitors and neighbors. "When we explain our management objectives and tell them that the stand will be regenerated, then people understand and say it's better than being developed!" says Edeburn. "We replant about half of the area that we harvest and the other half is regenerated naturally."

Prescribed Burning in the Forest

Although prescribed burning is not as significant a management tool as it is in fire-dependent natural communities in the Coastal Plain, the staff conducts some prescribed burning in certain sections of the Forest. "We know that Native Americans burned areas in the Piedmont to drive game and open up the woods, which contributed to the types of forests that were here historically, predominantly oak-hickory and open pine forests," explains Edeburn. "Because most fires are suppressed today, botanists like Norm Christensen and Bob Peet are detecting changes in some of the research plots they've studied for a long time. It appears that when oak and hickory trees die they're being replaced by a different set of understory trees, such as red maple, sweetgum, and yellow poplar, which would likely not be the case if there were periodic fires."

The staff conducts prescribed burns for teaching purposes, research, and to maintain habitat types in the Forest that may have developed under a historical fire regime. Fire crews periodically burn an 11-acre stand of longleaf pine in the Durham Division that was planted by Korstian. "Although the Forest is at the northwest end of the range for longleaf pine, Korstian picked the sandiest soil he could find in the Forest to grow an experimental plot of this species, and it seems to be thriving," says Edeburn.

The staff hope to conduct three or four understory burns every year and eventually burn about 50 or 60 acres every year. "It's unlikely that we'll introduce fire on the same scale as during the Native American period," says Edeburn. "But we intend to burn more acreage annually than we have in the past. We are constrained by a lot of factors, such as managing smoke because of development around the forest. There are places we would have burned 25 years ago that we can't burn now because of development."

Management of the Duke Forest creates a mosaic of forest cover types. The planted pine, open field, and surrounding hardwood stands in the Blackwood Division offer an array of conditions for various research projects. Duke University Photography.

Nicholas School student Erica Taecker assists with a prescribed burn in the Blackwood Division, Compartment 4, March 2006. Photo by Katherine Armstrong. Duke Forest Photo Collection.

Conservation Partnerships

As Duke Forest is one of the largest privately owned forests in the Triangle region, the Forest staff tries to stay tuned to all activity around the Forest that could impact it either beneficially or detrimentally, such as the construction of roads and developments. Edeburn has served on a number of committees that deal with land use policy and planning in the area. The Office worked with Orange County when the county conducted a rural character study before designating parts of the county Rural Buffer areas. And the Forest participated in making public comments when North Carolina Department of Transportation replaced the bridges over Mud Creek. (The Forest staff has an ongoing partnership with the New Hope Creek Advisory Committee, since the Korstian Division contains a core section of the creek's corridor protection plan.) Orange County commissioner Barry Jacobs says of the Forest: "Orange County residents surely love it, and we have a Lands Legacy Program in which I think we count on Duke Forest being part of the natural heritage."

The physical composition of the Forest has changed over time as the University has sold some portions and acquired additional land to round out boundaries or connect disjunct tracts. Several parcels of the Forest have been sold over time to Orange County and the Triangle Land Conservancy, a local land trust, to be preserved as open space. These tracts were typically small isolated parcels that were difficult to use effectively for teaching and research. Duke Power used to own a tract on the Haw River in Chatham County that the Forest helped manage through a cooperative agreement. In 1966, the company donated 1,360 acres of this property to the University and it officially became part of the Forest. But because of its distance from the university, the tract was rarely used for research, so the university began to consider selling it in the late 1990s. This ecologically significant tract protects a riparian buffer along the river, so the Triangle Land Conservancy started talking to Duke about protecting the property. "Tallman Trask, executive vice president of the University, agreed that because the property was a significant natural resource, Duke would not sell it

Vast stretches of fields and woodland with few houses or other development were common in the early years around the Duke Forest. Duke Forest Photo Collection.

In 2006 homesites dot the landscape around the Duke Forest. Duke Forest Photo Collection.

to the highest bidder, but would work with the Conservancy to protect it," recalls Edeburn. So, in 2004, with the assistance of the Triangle Land Conservancy, the property was sold to the State of North Carolina, to be preserved as part of the state park system.

"Duke Forest staff have been supportive of local conservation," says Jeff Masten, director of conservation strategies for the Triangle Land Conservancy. "They are community members, they sit on committees as stakeholders, and they influence the type and pace of conservation in areas around Duke Forest. Duke seeks to conserve the property that the community deems important in conservation plans, including recreational lands, lands that protect water quality, and property with natural heritage value."

Registered Natural Heritage Areas

In 2004, Duke University registered 1,220 acres of the Forest with the N.C. Natural Heritage Program, formalizing a conservation initiative that had begun twenty years earlier. "Back in 1980 when we were developing a management plan for the forest, Janet Ohmann was working on her master's project and identified a number of sections of the Forest that

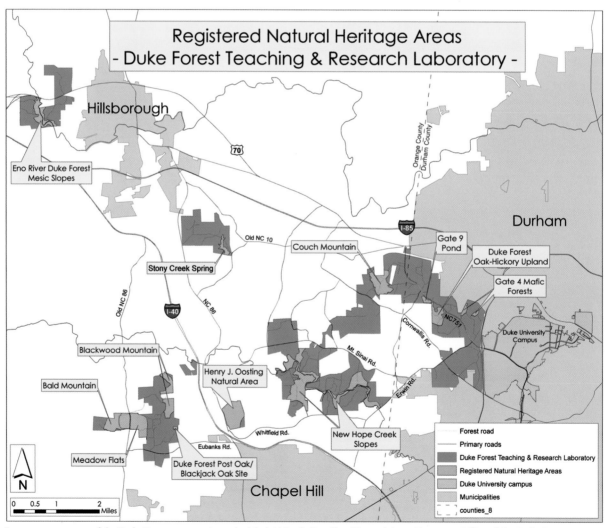

In 2004, 1,220 acres of the Duke Forest were registered with the North Carolina Natural Areas Program. Office of the Duke Forest.

contained exemplary plant communities or locally rare ecosystems," says Edeburn. "We were going to propose to the Duke administration to register these sites shortly after we identified them, but the political climate of the University at the time was not encouraging. We brought it up unofficially several times thereafter, but weren't getting a positive reaction from the administration. Then a couple of things converged: the Heritage program conducted ecological inventories of Durham and Orange County and confirmed that these were very significant sites; William Schlesinger, the dean of the Nicholas School, communicated strong support to the administration, and executive vice president Tallman Trask agreed that this was an acceptable recognition to pursue for these sites, because it would not preclude anything that the University might do in the future." Duke University is one of the few universities in North Carolina to have placed their property in such a program.

In managing these sections of the Forest, the staff essentially allows natural processes to occur there. The staff did not, for example, salvage any trees from the Heritage Sites that were damaged by Hurricane Fran. In the future, the staff may have to intervene occasionally, altering the management of these sites to try to control, for example, the spread of invasive species, which have become a greater problem.

"I think that the official recognition of these areas is a very positive and substantial step toward their long-term preservation," says Edeburn. "The registry formalized something that we had been aware of for many years, as we had always managed these unique parts of the forest to enhance their ecological value."

Management Challenges: The Growth of the Triangle

As the Triangle area of North Carolina continues to grow rapidly and more development is occurring around the Forest, the Forest's stewards are having to modify their management practices to be sensitive to neighboring landowners. "More people enter the Forest from their properties and begin to view the Forest as 'their backyard,' which can present some challenges," says Edeburn. The Forest management has to be sensitive about the visibility of some of its management programs, especially such activities as prescribed burning and timber harvesting.

"We're experiencing increasing problems with people who allow their dogs to run unleashed in the Forest," says Edeburn. The Forest initiated a leash-only policy after researchers and the staff observed that the free-running dogs were causing many environmental problems, such as destroying or disturbing the nests of ground-nesting birds such as ovenbirds, and eroding some of the fragile slopes along the

Signs indicating the guidelines for using the Duke Forest are located at each gate. Duke Forest Photo Collection.

creeks. As well, the Forest office was fielding complaints about aggressive dogs and damaged research plots. Forest policy requires people to walk dogs with a leash and the policy is posted on signs at every entrance to the Forest.

"The picnic sites in those days did a land office business. The sites were reserved months in advance, and keeping track of picnic keys and keeping the sites safe was time-consuming for both me and my crew. But that was more or less good old family recreation. The free-wheeling student body pursued a different kind of recreation, particularly along New Hope Creek. The fraternities played endless games with me and the Forest gates. It was an endless war to defeat the forest gates so they could get in and have a party down along the creek and foil my attempts to prevent this. One morning I got a call close to 3:00 a.m. from someone who said there was a tremendous fire on Piney Mountain. I figured it was a party, so I drove out there and the gates were down, so I drive on to Piney Mountain, and there was indeed a smoking campfire on top. There must have been 30 students naked as jay birds around the fire. I was so embarrassed, I just said, 'Well, don't let the fire get away.'"

– Fred White, former director of Duke Forest

"Unfortunately many people ignore those signs and let their dogs run freely around the Forest," laments Edeburn. "These owners are creating problems for everybody. The dogs are impacting wildlife and water quality. When you go to any drainage in the Forest there's a mud slick caused by dogs running up and down the bank. Some research forests have prohibited dogs entirely, so Duke Forest is somewhat unique because we do allow dogs. We hope that people will realize that this policy is in the best interests of both the Forest and the visitors, and abide by it."

The booming white-tailed deer population is a cause for concern as well. "The area's deer population is probably higher than it has ever been," says Edeburn. "Lack of natural predators, a decline in hunting, and increased pressure from development has not only resulted in increased numbers but concentrated them in and around areas like the Duke Forest. Research plots where seedling and herbaceous data is gathered indicate a major change in plant composition due to deer. Controlled hunting would reduce the population, but because of safety concerns for our students, faculty and recreational users, there is no easy fix. We are working on how we might address this issue."

It's Always the Weather

Severe weather, particularly ice storms and hurricanes, have battered the Forest over time. An ice or "glaze" storm in December of 1934 is documented in some of the Office's old photographs. Another ice storm, this one in December 2002, snapped the tops off many pine trees and caused extensive limb damage. The Forest was closed to the public through February 2003, and it cost about $55,000 in cleanup expenses, not including staff time.

Hurricane Fran was by far the most damaging storm to blow through the Forest. The eye of Fran hit the Triangle area early in the morning of September 6, 1996. After the storm had passed, Edeburn and his field crew of employees and students met at the Forest garage maintenance shop and began to assess the damage. "We were all amazed by the devastation," he recalls. "We counted more than 1,400 trees down over 35 miles of roads. We closed the various divisions of the forest for three to six months, depending on the damage, and spent most of that time trying working on hurricane cleanup."

Because the eye of the storm came closest to the Durham and Korstian Divisions, they suffered the most damage. And in part because Fran blew through during the growing season when the trees were still leafed out, the storm toppled many old hardwood trees, particularly in areas with saturated soils and northeast-facing slopes. "The largest tree that we found that was downed by Fran was a 250-year-old white oak," says Edeburn. "When we salvaged it, we cut out a section that is on display on the Shepherd Nature Trail."

Edeburn says this was the greatest management challenge he has faced during his tenure at the Forest. "We were dealing with so many issues like safety, gaining access, and assessing the amount of damage and deciding what to do about it," he says. "Not only did the hurricane damage the Forest, which caused us to lose a substantial amount of mature timber, it also damaged some of our facilities like roads, bridges, and structures. It cost about $200,000 to clean up and repair the roads and damage at research sites."

Loblolly pine covered with a glaze of ice following the storm of February 25, 1934. Durham Division, along N.C. Highway 751. Photo by C. F. Korstian. Duke Forest Photo Collection.

Ice-damaged pine plantation, Blackwood Division, Compartment 7, December 4, 2002. Photo by Judson Edeburn. Duke Forest Photo Archives.

The staff and an advisory committee developed a plan of action for responding to the storm damage; they decided to leave some areas undisturbed for research and identified other places where they could recoup economic losses by salvaging some of the downed trees. "We salvaged over 2 million board feet of timber after Hurricane Fran, on 540 acres," says Edeburn. "All of our regularly scheduled work was put on hold and we focused on recovery from Fran for more a year. We did not salvage in research areas where plots had been established to study long-term successional trends, nor did we employ conventional salvage in steep or wet areas. We hired helicopter crews to log in inaccessible places, and in places where that was the only feasible way to recover the most valuable timber without damaging the soil. It was a very expensive method, but we only removed the material that was profitable."

Of the total salvage, about 800,000 board feet was lifted out of 163 acres on the Forest by helicopter. In contrast, 400,000 board feet was salvaged after Hurricane Hazel in 1954.

Like other natural events, Hurricane Fran has become woven into the educational and research fabric of the Forest. "I think the interesting thing about that hurricane is that it has proven to be another lesson that we can learn from the Forest—about how disturbance is a natural part of forested ecosystems," says Edeburn. "The Forest is naturally recovering from that storm. Signs of recovery were all around after the storm, from new tree seedlings that popped up in gaps in the canopy, to animals that benefited from all the new growth that provided food. And many research projects have since developed that are examining various aspects of storm damage."

Damage resulting from Hurricane Fran, September 1996. Duke Forest Photo Collection.

Helicopter salvage logging was carried out on 163 acres on the Duke Forest after Hurricane Fran. Photo by Judson Edeburn. Duke Forest Photo Collection.

Forest Stewardship Council Forest Certification

In 2001 the Duke Forest participated in a dual certification project conducted through the Southern Center for Sustainable Forests. Along with North Carolina State University's College Forests it became one of the first university forests to become certified. Initially, both the Sustainable Forestry Initiative (SFI) and Forest Stewardship Council (FSC) certified the Forest. However, manpower and budget constraints have required limiting continued certification to one system, that of FSC, a nonprofit organization that promotes sustainable forestry.

"FSC has developed a set of principles and criteria for measuring long-term sustainability that are used as an international protocol for managing forests," explains Edeburn. "The protocol is not just focused on harvesting sustainably; it also emphasizes protecting biodiversity and soil and has criteria for land ownership and tenure. FSC staff audits the Forest according to these standards, and there's an annual review and then a five-year reassessment."

Students gather for a group shot after participating in a prescribed fire exercise on the Forest. Duke Forest Photo Collection.

Rewards of Forest Management

In addition to the benefits that come with a job that allows him to spend a lot of time outdoors, or at least some of his time, Edeburn considers his interactions with students to be one of the most rewarding parts of his job. "They always bring new energy and ideas to the Forest," he says. "We usually have two full-time student assistants during the summer, and between two and four that work part-time during the academic year. The students work on timber cruising and inventory, building and maintaining trails, or updating our management plan. They have helped us with our recreational survey, and set up plots for professors, worked on trails, and marked boundary lines.

"The Forest seems to have always had a very capable staff, and that has certainly been the case since I have been here. Forest technician Mike Burke, who joined the staff in 1985, knows the Forest as well as anyone and has an impressive set of skills.

Rainforest Alliance's forest auditing group SmartWood conducts an audit to standards set by the Forest Stewardship Council. Duke Forest Photo Collection.

Grounds maintenance supervisor George Pendergraft has been with us for 18 years and is expert in maintaining all of our roads, operating equipment and fabricating what ever needs to be repaired. Roberta (Bobbie) Reeves, our staff assistant, joined the Forest in 2001 and brought a wealth of knowledge about Duke's financial system. Bobbie has tremendous energy and initiative. Regan Lyons, a Nicholas School graduate with an excellent background, came on board this year and is responsible for our GIS system and data management. Everyone is versatile and willing to go the extra mile to get the job done."

As someone who has spent more time roaming around Duke Forest than just about anyone, Edeburn has a great affinity for many sections of the Forest. "One of the most fascinating things I do is observe changes in the Forest over time. I like to examine some of the old Forest photographs and then visit those areas to see how they look today. I like the Blackwood Division because it's got such diversity and interesting topography, with Bald Mountain and Blackwood Mountains, Meadow Flats, and the open fields. And there's a lot going on there both in areas that are undergoing terms of natural succession and in the managed stands, and a large number of research projects. No one can deny that the New Hope Creek Corridor is a very special place as well, with great diversity and scenic value."

Chapter 7
Community Perspectives

As the Triangle continues to grow, the ecological services provided by the Forest—clean water, clean air, and habitat for flora and fauna, become increasingly significant. There is no question that the Forest has become a treasured outdoor refuge for the Triangle community. Since the Forest was founded, Duke University has maintained an open-door policy, allowing the public and the university community to use it for passive recreation in addition to research.

The Forest as Open Space

"Where it does not conflict with other purposes of management, public use is desirable," wrote Clarence Korstian and William Maughan in the June 1935 *Forestry Bulletin*. "One of the outstanding needs in America today is the education of the people as to the proper use and care of their forests. One of the first steps in this direction is to encourage intelligent public use of the forests and thereby discourage their abuse."

In the 1930s, the Forest must have had a great appeal as an inexpensive form of entertainment. "It was the Depression that taught Durham the value of parks," writes Jean Bradley Anderson in *Durham County*. "The impulse to explore and enjoy the natural environment had obvious appeal when free

A pine seedling begins a new forest. Duke Forest Photo Collection.

entertainment was at a premium." But even in today's sunnier economic climate, the budget-conscious still flock to the Forest: in the *Durham Herald-Sun*'s 2006 "Reader's Choice Awards," readers selected Duke Forest as the "Best Free Fun."

Walk in one of the popular sections of the Forest any day of the week, any time of year, and you will inevitably meet other hikers, dog-walkers, runners, birders, or mountain bikers. Records from several Duke student master's projects show that between 180,000 and 200,000 people visit the Forest annually and that the number of visitors appears to grow at a constant rate of about 37 percent every year.

Duke Forest provides a greatly-valued expanse of open green space for the local community. "I'm heartened by the fact that the primary mission of Duke Forest is for research and education, and I think it's wonderful that Duke has it open for recreational use," says Rich Shaw, land conservation manager with Orange County's Environmental and Resource Department. "Up until 2001, there were no county parks in Orange County and I think Duke Forest really filled that need for the public."

For Shaw and others who worry about the future of green space in the rapidly growing Triangle region, Duke Forest represents a strategic foothold in the region's rural roots. "Duke is the largest landowner in Orange County and much of the 5,000 acres of Duke Forest land in the county is zoned as rural buffer through an agreement between Carrboro and Chapel Hill and Orange County," says Shaw. "This agreement created a buffer between these areas where there will be no public services like water and sewer lines. The fact that Duke University owns so much land in the area is very important to the rural character of that part of the county and it's kind of set the stage for the zoning that has occurred."

As just one example of the Forest's role in the conservation vision of Triangle communities and planners, the section of New Hope Creek that runs through the Korstian Division is considered a linchpin in the New Hope Corridor Open Space Master

Plan, a conservation and open space blueprint for the creek corridor from N.C. Highway 54 north and west to Erwin Road in Orange County. The town of Chapel Hill, city of Durham, and Durham and Orange Counties developed this cooperative plan in 1989 with the intent of protecting this key natural area and its water quality and offering open space and outdoor recreation to local communities.

A coalition of public and private conservation agencies scored a major victory for New Hope Creek in 2005 by protecting 110 acres in the Hollow Rock area, across Erwin Road from the Korstian Division. Alarmed by a proposed 43-acre development along Erwin and Pickett Roads, the Erwin Area Neighborhood Group (EANG) organized a grassroots campaign to raise the funds to protect the land for open space. Through a combination of conservation easements and acquisitions, a group of landowners, local government entities, and conservation agencies were able to protect more than 100 acres along the creek, connecting Duke Forest to a planned wildlife corridor and trail system along the creek that will extend to Jordan Lake. The group plans to establish the New Hope Preserve Park in the area, which will provide access to the eastern section of the Korstian Division. Although Duke Forest was not involved in this particular conservation effort, the Forest staff works closely with local environmental agencies in coordinating similar management and conservation efforts on lands bordering the Forest.

This involvement underscores how Duke Forest is woven into the Triangle's green space network. Jane Korest, City of Durham Environmental Planner, sees Duke Forest as a part of the "community's character." "As a planner, you have to be aware of the major assets of your community," she says. "What makes people want to live in Durham? What comes to mind? And I know Duke Forest is a treasured asset that comes to mind as a recreational and wildlife amenity. The relief and variation in that amount of woodland in the western part of the county is so much greater than any public park could provide, and of course

it has scientific benefit. I think Duke University deserves real credit and recognition for providing the community with the opportunity to get away and enjoy nature and have that experience in the woods."

Durham County Commissioner Becky Heron agrees: "As a city and a county, we need to consider the recreational activities and amenities that Duke Forest brings to the region and what that means for us. It's hard to put a dollar value on that. Without it, this community wouldn't be as desirable."

The Forest as Classroom

In the days of dwindling public school budgets and fewer wild places, Duke Forest offers students of all ages a cost-effective field trip destination. There are more than 13,000 student visits from the Triangle area and beyond to the Forest every year. The proximity to Duke University makes it an ideal field trip destination so students in the biology, botany, zoology, and other departments visit the Forest throughout the year for field trips, class projects, and laboratories. Students from the Nicholas School of the Environment and Earth Sciences are

Duke ACTION Science Camp has used the Duke Forest during the summer for a number of years. Duke Forest Photo Collection.

"I spent a lot of time in Duke Forest while I was an undergraduate at Duke, and some of my favorite memories are from trips I led for Durham students. I volunteered with a group called W.O.O.D.S. (Wilderness Outdoor Opportunities for Durham Students) for two years, and we offered environmental/nature education programs to children at rec centers around Durham. Most of the participants were from low-income families, and very few of them had ever had any outdoor experiences.

"Some of the most popular field trips we offered were to Duke Forest. We hiked different trails with the students. The Shepherd Nature Trail, which highlights damage and regrowth from Hurricane Fran on educational signs, was always a big hit. None of the students had any idea that actual wilderness existed in Durham, and they always talked about that trip for weeks to come. While I enjoyed hiking and working in Duke Forest myself, this is what sticks in my mind the most—it meant a lot that we could show those kids such a great natural area in their own backyards."

– Lauren Stulgis, Trinity 2001

New Hope Creek has been a popular location for photography and art classes.
Duke Forest Photo Collection.

"This week allowed us to really explore and learn about the watershed in which we live. It is now easy to see how much our actions affect the life in the stream, not only nearby but also farther downstream and in connecting creeks. A construction site running into a tributary of New Hope Creek will not only kill the life in that tributary but the life found all along the creek after the confluence of the two streams. We were able to identify a large variety of aquatic life which was very interesting. It is amazing how the number and diversity of species changed all within the same creek, and how varied the pollution levels were throughout the creek."

– Jill Freibele and Leslie O'Loughlin,
"Macroinvertebrates," from
"New Hope Creek: A Comprehensive Study,"
North Carolina School of Science and Math,
March 2000

"Day 4: Late Night—Rhododendron Bluff, Wooden Bridge, Mount Sinai. Located no life. Once it got dark the temperature dropped quickly and most likely the salamanders went to sleep in their warm beds like we should have done. We were not able to locate any other reptile and amphibian groups, even the frogs were not chirping. The cold weather deterred small animals from venturing out."

– Anne Chesky and Jonathan Wells, "Spotting
Salamanders: A Brief Look at the Habits
and Habitats of Salamanders," from
"New Hope Creek: A Comprehensive Study," North
Carolina School of Science and Math, March 2000

probably the most frequent student visitors to the Forest. And another universe of student users comes from local public schools, other universities, continuing education programs, summer camps, and Boy and Girl Scout troops.

The Forest has been utilized for many multidisciplinary studies in local schools. For several years, Joe Liles, head of the art department at the North Carolina School of Science and Math in Durham, engaged his students in a multidisciplinary study of New Hope Creek during the miniterm between semesters in the spring. Much of the students' fieldwork took place in and around the section of the creek that runs through the Korstian Division. During one miniterm the class traveled to the source of the creek in Orange County near Dodson's Crossroads. They photographed the creek, monitored aquatic life, met with Duke Forest staff, and studied birds, mammals, reptiles, and soil, snakes, and squirrels.

The Community Store in the Forest

Although no one alive today remembers Patterson's and Trice's general stores, their descendant, the old Hollow Rock country store, is a not-too-distant memory for many. The first Hollow Rock country store was built around 1930 by John Ransom Whitfield, according to a February 25, 2006 article in *The Durham News* by local historian Jim Wise. The store was located near the Erwin Road bridge over New Hope Creek, across the road from Duke Forest. The Whitfields rented the store to John Brown, and the store became a gathering place for the local community.

"The store served as a polling place and a handy stop for gas and groceries in days when town was distant, Erwin Road was dirt, and nights were dark enough to see the Aurora Borealis—as was recalled by the late musician Tommy Thompson, who in the early sixties frequented Friday-night picking sessions Brown hosted at the store," writes Wise. Thompson, a banjo player, formed a band called the Hollow Rock String Band and was one of the founding members of the Red Clay Ramblers. "It was a typical country store with a center aisle and shelves and counters on both sides," recalls Fred White. "They sold harnesses and automobile parts and clothes and groceries, and at the back was a pot-bellied stove surrounded by coke crates and that's where people gathered and played checkers. It was a delightful place."

When John Glenn Whitfield and his son Stanford took over the daily operations of the store in the late 1960s, which by then served as a gateway to the

The Hollow Rock Country Store, ca. 1971. Photo by Steve Heron.

Stan and Sue Whitfield, in the Hollow Rock Country Store. Photo by Steve Heron.

Korstian Division, they decided to build a larger store and gave the original store to potter Jan Gregg, who used it for a studio for close to 20 years. Today the New Hope Creek Corridor Advisory Committee is working to move the store back to its original location and convert it into an interpretive center for New Hope Preserve Park.

Putting a Price Tag on the Forest

Duke University's "accidental acquisition" of Duke Forest has precipitated a long-running debate among members of the University community: How do you measure the value of the Forest? Inevitably, the answer to the question depends on who you ask. Since the mid-1960s, there have been several crisis points for the Forest when people from both the University and the local community eyed the property as more of a financial or real estate asset than an educational resource.

A potential impact to the Forest occurred in the mid-1960s, when Fiber Industries, a subsidiary of Celanese Corporation that manufactured synthetic polyester, proposed building a new plant on New Hope Creek upstream from the Korstian Division, near Turkey Farm Road in Chapel Hill. The company purchased a 450-acre tract north of Chapel Hill and requested that Orange County rezone the area to an industrial classification for the construction of the plant.

"This was the first real threat to Duke Forest from outside the Duke community," says Judd Edeburn. "Many faculty members from Duke University and UNC became involved in opposing this proposal because of the potential impact on the creek and the research taking place in the Korstian Division. There was concern that the plant could degrade the water quality in New Hope Creek, as well as the company's potential interest in acquiring Duke Forest land. So faculty and other members of the community organized a grassroots campaign: They talked to county commissioners, wrote letters, and requested that the State designate New Hope Creek as a research stream."

Billy (B. B.) Olive, a Durham attorney and Duke alumnus, played a key role in the opposition. In June 1969, he wrote an "Open and Urgent letter" to the Duke trustees and administration, saying: "Water, air and thermal pollution all stand as present and potential threats." Citing Duke Forest's immense value as a research site and calling it an "invaluable and irreplaceable asset," Olive concluded his letter with an impassioned tone: "Dead fish, dead plants and dead science cannot be revived and cannot speak for humanity."

The Duke administration and Board of Trustees also entered the fray. In a July 14, 1969 letter to Fred White, who was administrative director of the Forest, Barnes Woodhall, the chancellor pro tem, noted that although the University "is not interested in denying the opportunity of private industry development in this region of the State," it also "has the task, however,

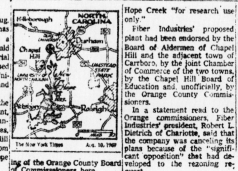

Fiber Industries decides to cancel plans for its proposed manufacturing plant on New Hope Creek. Office of the Duke Forest.

of protecting its own investment in its resources for education and research." Woodhall continued that the University's position had been outlined in a memorandum from University provost Marcus Hobbs from July 2 that noted that the proposed plant's wastewater should be emptied into New Hope Creek east of the Korstian Division, "at a point where there is already considerable waste effluent."

In the face of this concerted opposition, Fiber Industries scrapped their plans for the new plant in the summer of 1969. Edeburn credits Olive for his instrumental role in fighting off the potential threat. "B. B. Olive was immersed in defending the creek and the Forest," recalls Edeburn. "He helped rally the community and the University around the whole fight, and if he hadn't been so vociferous, the plant could have been built."

The Community Debates Preservation or Change

At times Duke University itself has considered alternative uses for the Forest. Former Duke Forest director Fred White wryly noted in a 2003 interview that discussions about selling portions of the Forest arise periodically in the University community "almost like a celestial event." One of the most contentious public debates about the fate of the Forest erupted in 1986, when Duke University hired the Urban Land Institute (ULI), an independent research organization, to recommend a management strategy for the University's land holdings based on their projections about future land use in the Triangle area. The ULI team interviewed more than 100 members of the campus community and in February 1987, presented their report to the University's Board of Trustees. The report acknowledged Duke Forest's value as a research site, but noted that:

> the panel finds it difficult to justify the preservation of all forest lands in their current state. It sees the most immediate development potential in the Durham division of Duke Forest at the intersection of the US 15-501 bypass and NC 751, where a research park, planned residential community, and small specialty shopping center could be built. Any development in these areas should be environmentally sensitive.

Then-president of Duke University, Dr. H. Keith H. Brodie, recalled in a 2003 interview that many people immediately concluded that the Forest was doomed. "The public began to think that the university administration was going to sell the Forest, and develop it and change it. That was not the intent, but it became the public perception."

"The public reaction to the ULI report was very negative," recalls Edeburn. "When the press got wind of it, some community members headed by the late Bill Nealy formed a group called 'Save Duke Forest' that organized the public opposition to the forest." Nealy, an avid mountain biker, kayaker, and talented artist who probably explored and mapped every inch of Duke Forest, was quoted in an article in the *New York Times* on November 15, 1987, saying: "We're not rabid antidevelopment people. We are basically trying to sell Duke Forest to Duke University." The article noted that "some 6,500 people [had] signed a petition requesting that any development within the forest be kept moderate in scale."

Changes in water quality occur as development increases. Duke Forest Photo Collection.

In fact, the University administration never officially or publicly endorsed the development suggestions proposed by ULI. In the summer of 1987, University officials formed a task force called the Land Resources Committee (LRC) in order to develop a strategic land management plan for the University's

"The forested spaces beyond West Campus contribute far more to the perceived quality of the university and to the psychological and physical well-being of its faculty, staff, students and visitors, than could be made up by money from its sale. There are certain symbols of any institution, the value of which cannot be calculated in economic terms. Along with the chapel, the Duke Gardens, and the architecture itself, Duke University's forest is part of its identity, a legacy of the founding process which must not be further sacrificed to short-term economic contingency."

– James Applewhite, in a letter to Professor Dale Randall, Academic Use Subcommittee of the Land Resources Committee, March 10, 1988

noncampus property, the bulk of which was contained within Duke Forest. Trustees, administrators, faculty, students, and alumni comprised the LRC and its subcommittees. "It would be the Academic Uses Subcommittee—charged with determining the academic and research value of Duke Forest—that carried the greatest responsibility," wrote Harold Steen in a 1989 edition of *FOREM*. "After all, the only real argument against selling off the forest was that it had even greater value intact as part of the university's scientific and educational programs."

For about a year, members of the LRC's Academic Uses Subcommittee interviewed members of the campus community and beyond and compiled reports about the numerous historic and current research and educational projects in the Forest. In its final report released in the spring of 1989, the LRC divided the Forest into different categories that dictated future land use based on factors such as research use and ecological and historical significance. Sections of the property that had tremendous long-term research value, such as the Oosting Natural Area, were placed off-limits to development,

This seasonally wet upland area in the Blackwood Division provides important habitat. Duke Forest Photo Collection.

Mill sites, cemeteries, and old home sites provide important clues about our history. Photo by Ida Phillips Lynch.

Locating a landfill in the Blackwood Division would have disrupted research. Duke Forest Photo Collection.

while areas east of U.S. 15-501 were designated as no longer part of Duke Forest and made available for campus expansion.

Although the LRC recommendations did not permanently protect any sections of the Forest, the entire ULI/LRC process worked to galvanize community support behind protecting the Forest. "At the end of the day, the ULI/LRC experience resulted in bringing in many people that were against selling and developing the Forest," says Brodie.

The Orange County Landfill Controversy

On the heels of the LRC report, another conflict emerged that strained town-gown relations between Duke University and local governments. In October 1989, the Landfill Owners' Group, a governmental team representing Chapel Hill, Carrboro, and Orange County, began the lengthy process of searching for a suitable site for the next Orange County landfill, as the existing landfill on Eubanks Road in Chapel Hill was thought to be nearing capacity. In January 1991 the group released a list of sixteen candidate sites, and in April of that year, they added a name to the list—Site OC-17—which comprised more than half of Duke Forest's Blackwood Division, located next to the Eubanks Road landfill.

Although the Blackwood Division is not as heavily used by the public as the Durham and Korstian Divisions, it has been utilized for some of the most intensive and long-term research projects in the Forest. At the time of the landfill debate, William Schlesinger was "one of 22 researchers working on a project to measure the amount of pollution absorbed by trees," according to an article in the (Raleigh) *News and Observer* of March 8, 1995. As well, Norm Christensen was participating in a NASA-funded project to map vegetation from space by using aircraft satellite and space shuttles, including *Endeavour*, which collected data from the Forest in the summer of 1994. The landfill construction would have doomed these projects. "Researchers who were getting major grants for using the Blackwood Division were concerned about beginning their work in the Forest with the prospect that their research site could be gone in a year or two," explains Edeburn.

Once again, an outspoken citizens group rallied around the Forest. A group calling itself Stop Eubanks Area Landfill (SEAL) took an active role in the public hearing process. "They wrote letters and spoke passionately at every public hearing emphasizing the importance of the Duke Forest for research, teaching, and open space," recalls Edeburn. "They were an extremely important part of the process." The group included some of the longtime defenders of the Forest, such as Bill Nealy and B. B. Olive.

In the end, the very research that the landfill threatened proved to be the Forest's salvation. At the time of the debate the U.S. Department of Energy (DOE) was considering the Forest as a potential site for the FACE project. In 1995, Duke University granted a research easement to the DOE on a 93-acre parcel in the Blackwood Division to use for the research site, effectively blocking Orange County from exercising eminent domain and possibly condemning the area for the landfill. In June of 1996, Duke University granted another research easement

Jeff Pippen stands in the middle of the Concrete Bridge Road, rattling off the names of birds he hears. It's the first day of June, and the forest is full of birdsong as many birds are at the peak of their breeding fervor. Pippen, a research associate at the Nicholas School, gives this group of bird enthusiasts some tips on remembering the birds' calls. "Blue-gray gnatcatcher—it squeaks," he says. "Jib-jib-jib—that's a goldfinch. Eastern towhee—drink your tea! Prairie warbler—up the scale. Hooded warbler—weedle, zeet zeet. Now there's a cool bird singing!" he exclaims, and we hear the warble of the yellow-breasted chat, the largest warbler species in North America. We spot the bright yellow bird perched in a tree on the edge of a young pine stand. This is a rare treat because chats are notoriously sulky and will taunt you from the interior of an impenetrable thicket, staying just out of view.

Pippen has been conducting annual bird surveys in the Forest since 2003 in order to determine what bird species utilize the Forest. Although it is still too early to draw conclusive results from his study, Pippen hopes that with enough time the surveys will provide information about trends in the Forest's bird diversity and will reveal whether the diversity is being affected by changing environmental factors, such as increased development. Pippen conducts the surveys every season, and typically tallies about 40 to 50 species during the fall and spring migration, when neotropical migrants pass through the Forest as they journey to their breeding or wintering grounds.

Pippen and other naturalists delight in the Forest's many birding, butterflying, and general "naturalizing" opportunities. "Duke's open access policy is really nice for people who want to get out and go birding without having to drive hundreds of miles," he says. "Here you can essentially go birding right out your back door. It's a great resource for researchers as well as for avid avocational birders. And it's great for birds themselves. A lot of research has shown that a number of bird species need intact forested areas that are not broken into little pieces in order to successfully breed. Duke Forest definitely fits the bill."

A bird checklist is available for download at the Duke Forest Web site: www.env.duke.edu/forest/.

to NASA on roughly 365 acres in the division that strengthened the case against future condemnation.

The granting of the easements signaled to researchers that Duke University was committed to protecting this valuable research forest. "The only thing that Duke could do to insure the preservation of the Blackwood Division was to establish the easements," says Edeburn. "This was controversial, but I think researchers can now be confident that they will have the ability to continue long-term projects and have data available in the future. It was a milestone for the Duke trustees to agree to that kind of an easement with the federal government."

As well, the community's outpouring of support signified a great affection for the Forest. "One thing about all these Forest battles is that for the most part, the citizens who started the fight maintained the fight," says Olive. "There is definitely a large group of citizens here who really appreciate Duke Forest and are willing to sacrifice their time and go to battle for the Forest. I think that's very significant. There's something beautiful and wonderful in the composition or makeup of those people interested in the Forest. It's not superficial: It's deep. It's very deep. I think that makes all the difference."

The Forest as Inspiration

The Forest has always provided people with a place to retreat, escape, and observe. In the "old days" the Forest provided community gathering places, where people swam in New Hope Creek's deep tea-colored pools and picnicked under the gnarled trees on top of Piney Mountain. Today wildlife enthusiasts trek on the trails in springtime, peering to catch a glimpse of a scarlet tanager and standing utterly still when they encounter a barred owl staring intently at them. Runners pound the trails, chasing the endorphin rush and exorcising stress. "People depend on it for all kinds of recreation—fishing, hiking, picnicking—or just to get away and wander in the woods," says Jean

He is running in Duke Forest,
secure in his air of separate thought.
The trees to his left are cut,
where a roadbed gleams its rails
and seals the houses beyond, like a town
he has known and lost. The sound
from there is banging on an anvil, dogs
in their pens chase him with their baying—
as if the dust wanted voice. One hand,
huge enough to close him in its fist,
follows like a ghostly uncle, finger out
to touch. Other lives pursue, like wasps
swarming after. Dust-devil energies spin, potencies
in crockery bits wait near his feet, tiger
lilies crouch ahead, waiting for their spring—
now that the house is gone, with only
his steps, in a yard that once was swept.
Where low sun in its long, underwater
gloom washes about columns of pines,
he smells resin, that reminds him of an earlier
life. He feels forgotten speech flooding behind
his lips, feels wishes and memories, chemises
and masonry, iron spikes driven in by hand.
From the roadbed he inhales spilled oil,
the creosoted ties, vacuum after the locomotive's
passage like the odor of a rifle shot.
The backyard farmer is still banging upon
an axle, as if he shod a whole cavalry;
the spader of spring earth is turning up
earthworms and earlier. The unsatisfied,
lost lives swarm in their particles, like gnats
in summer air. They sting him and soothe him.
His emotions stream from their pressure
like a banner. Like a flag he is carrying, running.

– James Applewhite, "The Runner, Pursued"
Reprinted by permission of Louisiana
State University Press from *Lessons in
Soaring: Poems by James Applewhite*.
©1989 by James Applewhite.

William Nealy's quirky maps were popular with many people. Courtesy of William Nealy.

Bradley Anderson. "It's attractive to botanists, photographers, and birders. It's a many-faceted resource for respite from the daily grind. I think it's the wild, untapped and unchanged character that people like so much."

For artists, the Forest can be a wellspring of inspiration. Joe Liles, head of the art department at the North Carolina School of Science and Math in Durham, says that he's "always felt a spiritual connection to the section of New Hope Creek that runs through Duke Forest," and this bond is apparent in both his screen prints and elegant black-and-white photos that adorn the walls of his studio and offices of the school. William Nealy memorialized his

passion for the place in a series of hand-drawn quirky maps published by Menasha Ridge Press that feature tips for bikers.

When the Nasher Museum of Art at Duke University opened in 2005, the opening exhibit, *The Forest: Politics, Poetics and Practice*, capitalized on Duke's wooded campus. Artist Patrick Dougherty built an enormous sculpture called *Side Steppin'* that "consists of 11 hut-like forms which constitute a kind of garden path to the front door of the museum," explains Dougherty. "The sculpture is made primarily of red maple saplings that were considered interlopers in a new pine forest in Duke Forest. Volunteers and a landscape crew gathered the saplings and transported them to the museum where volunteers helped remove the summer leaves and prepare the saplings for use in the sculpture." Dougherty says that the sculpture "embodies the view that a connection to nature is restorative and an important component in a human's sense of well-being." Calling Duke Forest "a place of respite for the entire community," he believes that *Side Steppin'* is "a touchstone for the experience of leaving the blacktop and walking unencumbered into the depths of the Duke Forest itself."

Dougherty is not alone in viewing Duke Forest as an ideal setting for his own form of creative recreation. While serving as the founding director of the Institute of the Arts at Duke University, poet and English professor James Applewhite and his students immersed themselves in a semester-long study of abstract expressionist painters: Willem de Kooning, Mark Rothko, Jackson Pollock, and others. The uninhibited energy of Pollock's famed drip paintings sparked a creative surge in Applewhite. "At that time I was running every day and I thought I'd make a journal of the day's run, but then I decided that I would make a book length poem about whatever came to me during the day's run," Applewhite recalls. "Many times I wrote poems in my head while I was running. I would come back home and have the lines or key rhymes or concepts in my head and write them

Artist Patrick Dougherty constructs his Side Steppin' *sculpture for the opening of the Nasher Museum of Art. Duke Forest Photo Collection.*

down. I was thinking of Jackson Pollock's 'action painting' at the time, and I decided I wanted to write 'action poetry,' which was as close to drip painting as I could achieve in words."

Over the next year and a half, Applewhite wrote an entire collection of poems that germinated in his daily runs in Duke Forest and along the Eno River. Many of the verses were published in 1988's *River Writing: An Eno Journal* and in 1989's *Lessons in Soaring*. Almost 20 years later, Applewhite can remember the exact road, or hill, or glade of trees that spawned the poems. As we talked about his writing in July 2006, he read each poem and reminisced

about the scene in the Forest that helped bring the poems to life. Applewhite said that sometimes the Forest evoked what he calls the "topographical unconsciousness," when a place or scene unearths a long-submerged memory. He recalled: "In 'The Runner, Pursued,' I was running on the trail past Gate 13, which at first is flat and piney and runs beside the railroad. There were small houses by the railroad and they reminded me of the town where I grew up. It seemed that this side of the railroad was the present and that side was the past. At different times, Duke Forest has offered me windows on the past. In this poem the white, sandy trails between the brown pine needles reminded me of emotions from my childhood and earlier life. Memories from earlier in my life are embodied in the forest, in the land underfoot."

Applewhite recalled a day when he ran into the Forest from Gate 23 off Mt. Sinai Road, crossed the Wooden Bridge, emerged on Whitfield Road, and then looped back into the Forest through Gate 25. As he neared the end of his run on the Big Bend Fire Trail, the landscape inspired an idea: "Coming out in the open, this poem hit me. I'd come out of the green forest to this opening where there were some dead trees and I saw some woodpeckers. The air felt thin, like looking into space." "Slender Pines in Smoky Light" captures this moment in the amber of the lines:

> They point up through this
> air turning blue before space,
> move with the ridge as
> it turns, continue their wiry
> green though behind them others
> whiten, bare without bark,
> hollowed by woodpeckers.

Like many Forest enthusiasts, Applewhite perceives the landscape as a web, where the strands of human activity and natural processes intersect in infinite ways. He remembers walking into the Forest off of Highway 751 by an area that had recently been burned in preparation for harvest. He found the remnant of a chimney and a hearth from an old house, and looking closer, melted glass fragments in the ashes. He wrote "Vision in Ashes" about this experience, part of which reads:

> Deer tracks pointed toward a slope where,
> Sure enough, a rough memorial was tumbled.
> Two piles of stones with their eight paces
> Between had been chimneys. I looked across
> Charred earth and the carcasses of saplings.
> I found a dry well, with rim-rocks knocked
> Down its throat. Instead of water, my loitering
> About caught at two lumps of stuff once melted
> On stones like an altar.

A runner enjoys a sunny winter day in the Korstian Division. Photo by Richard Broadwell. Duke Forest Photo Collection.

Applewhite recalls how the scene in the Forest prompted an internal conversation about the connection between humans and nature: "It set off that dialectic when you think about the natural and the cultivated, the raw and the cooked, the landscape and human inscription in it," he recalls. "And it reminded me also that all of this forest is essentially second or third growth, but it used to be farmland. So it holds even more interest, knowing that first it was virgin countryside and then it was cut and farmed and now it's forest again. It's a testament in part to the resilience and persistence of life. Nature has this amazing capacity to recover."

Catawba rhododendron (Rhododendron catawbiense) *near bluffs above New Hope Creek. Photo by Joe Liles. North Carolina School of Science and Mathematics.*

"The Forest is one of Duke's most important futures … both from the point of view of our history and our research opportunities, and how it becomes an amazing example of the ways green space can be preserved. The Duke Forest is a showcase of multiple, successful ways to manage land in the middle of a rapidly growing urban environment and is part of an institution that sees it as a very important priority to preserve."

– Dr. Nannerl O. Keohane, president
of Duke University 1993–2004

Appendix
A Visitor's Guide to Duke Forest

D UKE FOREST IS OPEN TO THE GENERAL PUBLIC for a variety of recreational activities, including hiking, biking, horseback riding, fishing, and picnicking. The 7,050-acre Forest is a favorite destination for birders, photographers, botanists, and wildlife enthusiasts. More than 45 entrances provide access into the Forest's six divisions in Alamance, Durham and Orange counties. A 75-mile network of gravel roads and 11 miles of footpaths crisscross the Forest's six divisions, providing foot, bike, and horse access into the Forest.

Because the Forest is managed primarily as a research and teaching facility, public recreation must not conflict with teaching and research projects. The Office of the Duke Forest must approve group activities in advance. Visit the Office of Duke Forest Web site (http://www.env.duke.edu/forest) to access a wealth of additional information, including downloadable maps and brochures and information about events and volunteer activities.

Location and Maps

Detailed maps showing all forest roads, foot trails, creeks, and topographic contours may be purchased from the Office of the Duke Forest. Visit the Web site to download and purchase maps.

Hiking/Running

Access roads and trails throughout the Forest provide opportunities for running and hiking. The roads and trails vary in length from under one mile to more than five miles, with variable topography. Hikers may also use the posted footpaths and are encouraged to visit the 0.8-mile self-guided Shepherd Nature Trail located off of N.C. 751 at Gate C. (See description below under "Nature Study.") Footpaths can be found in the Eno, Korstian, and Durham Divisions and are posted with yellow "Designated Access Area" signs. There are no water sources or restroom facilities along the Forest's foot paths and roadways (with the exception of the Al Buehler Trail, which has water fountains).

Detailed maps showing all roads and foot trails on the Forest are available to the public on the Web site. The three-mile Al Buehler Cross Country Trail has a graded course and winds through the woods around the Washington Duke Inn and Golf Course. For downloadable maps of the course, please see the Web site.

The Forest is closed to vehicular traffic, except for Duke Forest staff and researchers. Some sections of the Forest's roads may not be suitable for foot traffic due to the large size of the road gravel used. Please

stay on the maintained roads and designated trails, as bush-whacking and off-trail use can damage vegetation, soil stability, and possibly harm research and teaching areas.

Nature Study

The Forest is a perfect place to study and enjoy the Piedmont's diversity of flora and fauna. The seasons bring a great variety of sights and sounds. Sections of the Forest, particularly on rich slopes along the creeks, are noted for wonderful springtime wildflower displays with trilliums, trout lilies, and irises. Fall offers colorful foliage and perfect temperatures. Winter is a great time to study the topography and human history of the landscape, as old roads and agricultural fields are visible during that season.

The Shepherd Nature Trail is located in the Durham Division off N.C. 751 at Gate C. This self-guided 0.8-mile-long trail winds through a variety of habitats typical of North Carolina's Piedmont, including bottomland forests, rocky hilltops, and riparian areas. Visitors can learn about tree species, forest processes, past inhabitants, and current research through interpretive signs along the trail. An interpretive brochure is also available on the Web site. Hurricane Fran altered this section of the forest: in some sections of the trail more than 80 percent of the canopy trees were blown down. The trail is named for the family who farmed this property before Duke University purchased the land.

Picnicking

Duke Forest maintains two picnic shelters off of N.C. Highway 751, which are available to rent. To make shelter reservations, contact the Office of Duke Forest at (919) 613-8013 or visit the Web site.

Bobby Ross Jr. Memorial Shelter (Gate C)

Located at the trailhead of the Shepherd Nature Trail, this shelter is an ideal location for outdoor educational activities. The site offers a picnic shelter with a fireplace and four large picnic tables (50–75 person capacity) and a grill. The site does not have an outhouse, electricity, or running water. Call the Office of the Duke Forest for current rental rates.

R. L. Rigsbee Shelter (Gate F)
This site includes a picnic shelter and tables (50 person capacity), grill, outhouse, and volleyball court (net and ball not provided). The site offers electricity and lights but no running water. Call the Office of the Duke Forest for current rental rates.

Fishing
Fishing is permitted in the Forest for visitors with a valid local fishing license who follow local regulations. The New Hope Creek in the Korstian Division offers several popular fishing spots.

Horseback Riding
More than thirty miles of forest roads are available for horseback riding in the Forest. Due to the fragile nature of soils, the Forest contains no earthen trails suitable for horseback riding. The Forest does not maintain any horse stables; however, several commercial stables are located nearby.

Biking
More than 75 miles of roads are available for biking in the Duke Forest. Bikers are also welcome to use the 3.4 miles of prepared surface trail that winds through the woods around the Duke University Golf Course. Due to the fragile nature of forest soils, the Duke Forest contains no single track dirt trails suitable for mountain biking.

Forest Environment
The Forest lies near the eastern edge of the North Carolina Piedmont plateau and supports a cross section of habitats typical of the lower Piedmont of the Southeast. A variety of timber types, plant species, soils, topography, and past land use conditions are represented. More detailed information about the Forest's environment can be found on the Web site.

Wildlife Viewing in Duke Forest
The Duke Forest is a perfect destination for wildlife viewing throughout the year. Observant hikers can be rewarded with a variety of seasonal events, including spring and fall bird migrations and frog and salamander breeding activity in late winter and early spring. Given the diversity of wildlife in the Forest, taking a field guide or two on your hike can be invaluable. (See the "Further Reading" list below.) As well, the Duke Forest Web site offers downloadable brochures and species checklists for butterflies and birds found in the Forest.

Further Reading
Forest Ecology
Godfrey, Michael. *Field Guide to the Piedmont: The Natural Habitats of America's Most Lived-In Region, from New York City to Montgomery, Alabama.* Chapel Hill: University of North Carolina Press, 1997.

Kricher, John C., and Gordon Morrison. *A Field Guide to Ecology of Eastern Forests, North America.* New York: Houghton Mifflin, 1988.

Trail Guides
Dery, Maia. *Adventure Guide to the Triangle.* Winston-Salem: John F. Blair Publisher, 2005.

deHart, Allen. *Trails of the Triangle: Over 200 Hikes in the Raleigh/Durham/Chapel Hill Area.* Winston-Salem: John F. Blair Publisher, 1997.

Bird Identification
Alderfer, Jonathan, *National Geographic Complete Birds of North America.* Washington, D.C.: National Geographic Society, 2005.

Peterson, Roger Tory. *A Field Guide to the Birds of Eastern and Central North America.* New York: Houghton Mifflin, 2002.

Potter, Eloise F., James F. Parnell, Robert P. Teulings, and Ricky Davis. *Birds of the Carolinas,* 2nd ed. Chapel Hill: University of North Carolina Press, 1986.

Sibley, David Allen. *The Sibley Field Guide to Birds of Eastern North America.* New York: Knopf, 2003.

Plant Identification
Justice, William S., C. Ritchie Bell, and Anne H. Lindsey. *Wild Flowers of North Carolina*, 2nd ed. Chapel Hill: University of North Carolina Press, 2006.

Petrides, George A., and Janet Wehr. *A Field Guide to Eastern Trees*, 2nd ed. Peterson Field Guides. New York: Houghton Mifflin, 1998.

Fauna Field Guides
Martof, Bernard S., William M. Palmer, Joseph R. Bailey, and Julian R. Harrison III. *Amphibians and Reptiles of the Carolinas and Virginia.* Chapel Hill: University of North Carolina Press, 1989.

Webster, William David, James F. Parnell, and Walter C. Biggs Jr. *Mammals of the Carolinas, Virginia, and Maryland.* Chapel Hill: University of North Carolina Press, 2004.

Get Involved

As a Duke Forest volunteer, you can be directly involved in improving the Forest and helping us to carry out our teaching and research mission. The Forest's many volunteer opportunities provide an opportunity to work on a long-term or short-term commitment, work indoors or in the field with staff and other volunteers, and learn new skills. Visit the Web site to learn more about current volunteer opportunities.

Duke University
Office of the Duke Forest
Box 90332
Durham, NC 27708-0332
Phone: (919) 613-8013
Fax: (919) 684-8741
E-mail: dukeforest@duke.edu
Web site: www.dukeforest.duke.edu

New Hope Creek after a rare heavy snowfall. Photo by Joe Liles. North Carolina School of Science and Mathematics.

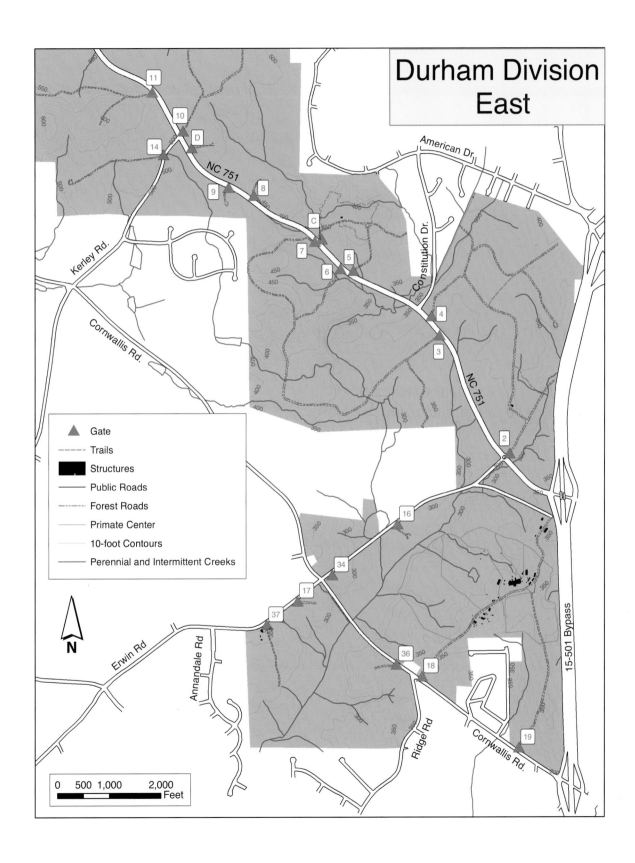

Durham Division East

Legend:
- ▲ Gate
- Trails
- Structures
- Public Roads
- Forest Roads
- Primate Center
- 10-foot Contours
- Perennial and Intermittent Creeks

0 500 1,000 2,000 Feet

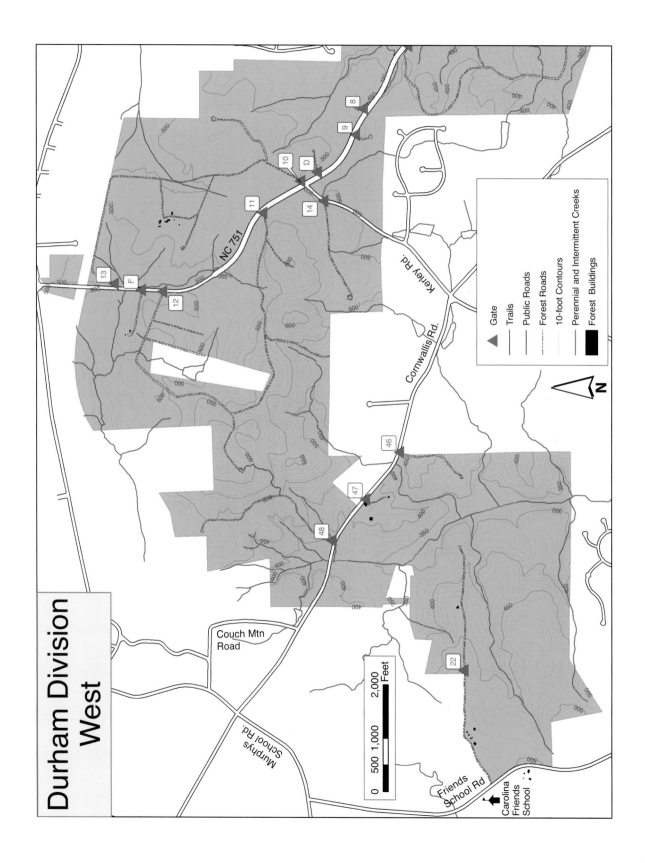

Durham Division West

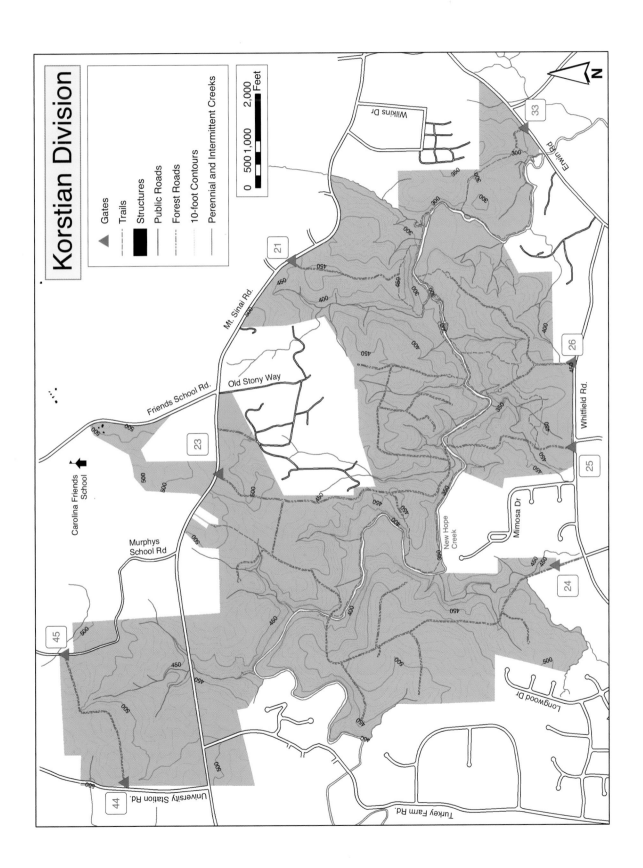

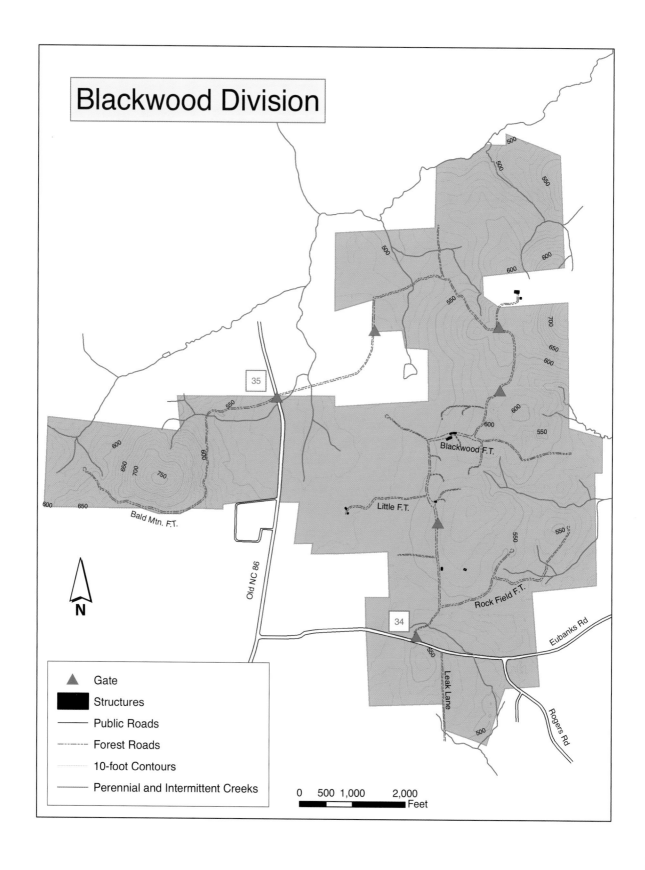

Blackwood Division

Gate

Structures

Public Roads

Forest Roads

10-foot Contours

Perennial and Intermittent Creeks

0   500 1,000   2,000
Feet

N

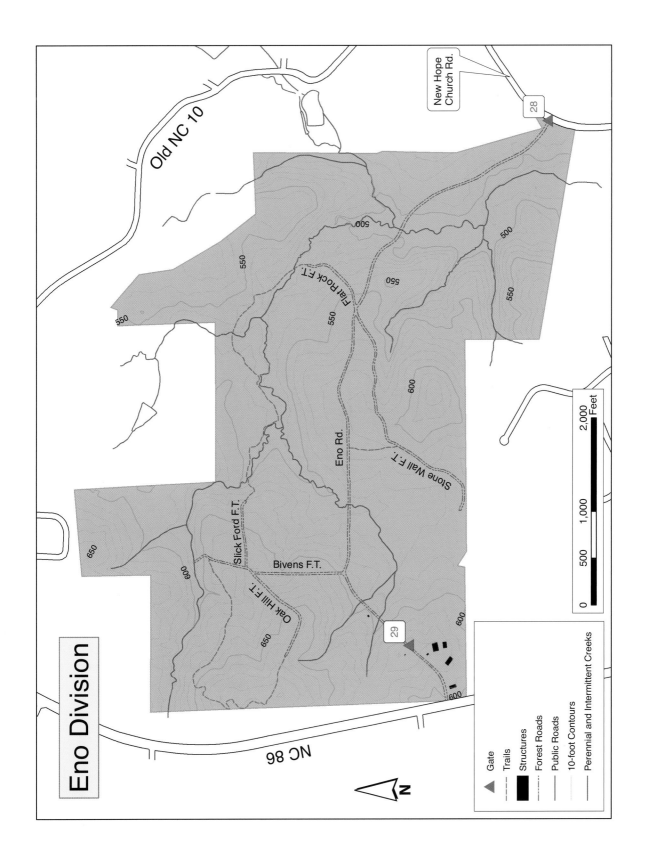

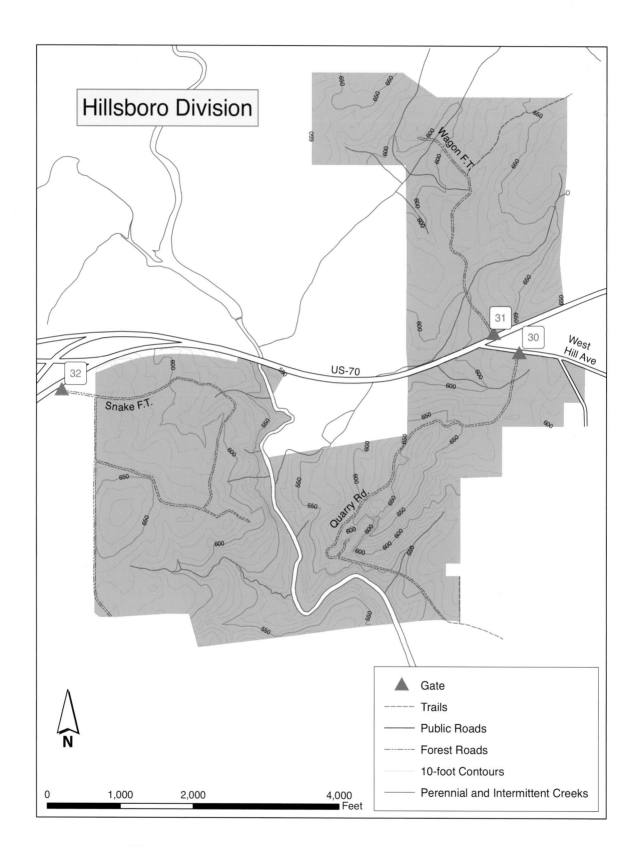

Hillsboro Division

Bibliography

Anderson, Jean Bradley. "A Community of Men and Mills." *Eno Journal 7* (1978): 30–33.

———. *Durham County: A History of Durham County, North Carolina.* Durham: Duke University Press in association with the Historic Preservation Society of Durham, Inc., 1990.

Applewhite, James. *Lessons in Soaring: Poems by James Applewhite.* Baton Rouge: Louisiana State University Press, 1989.

Ashe, W. W. "Suggestions Concerning the Forest Lands within and Adjoining the Campus of Duke University, Durham, North Carolina." Durham: Office of the Duke Forest, Duke University, 1926.

Boyd, William Kenneth. *The Story of Durham: City of the New South.* Durham: Duke University Press, 1925.

Browning, Hugh Conway. *More Orange County, North Carolina, Families: Breeze, Brown, Cabe, Johnston, Latta, Lockhart, McCown, Patterson, Piper, Shields, Strayhorn, etc.* Chapel Hill: Davie Poplar Chapter, NSDAR, 1968.

Christensen, Norman L. "Landscape History and Ecological Change." *Journal of Forest History* (July 1989): 116–124.

Craig, Rev. D. I. *A Historical Sketch of New Hope Church, in Orange County, N.C.* Reidsville: S. W. Paisley, Steam Job Printer, 1886.

Daniel, I. Randolph, Jr. *An Archaeological Survey of Portions of Orange County, North Carolina.* Research Report 12. Chapel Hill: University of North Carolina, Research Laboratories of Archaeology, 1994.

Davis, R. P. Stephen, Jr., et al. *Excavating Occaneechi Town: Archaeology of an Eighteenth-Century Indian Village in North Carolina.* Chapel Hill: University of North Carolina, Research Laboratories of Archaeology. Web edition 1998, 2003. http://www.rla.unc.edu/dig/ (accessed June 7, 2006).

Duke University. *Bulletin of Duke University* 4, no. 4 (1932).

———. *Duke University Alumni Register* 17, no. 3 (1931).

Durden, Robert F. *The Dukes of Durham: 1865-1929.* Durham: Duke University Press, 1975.

———. *The Launching of Duke University: 1924-1949.* Durham: Duke University Press, 1993.

Edeburn, Judson, and Richard Broadwell. "Management of the Duke Forest." Durham: Office of the Duke Forest, Duke University, December 2004.

Engstrom, Mary Claire. "The Hartford Mill Complex During the Revolution." *Eno Journal 7* (1978): 52–60.

Few, William Preston. "The Beginnings of an American University." Few Papers and Addresses. Duke University Archives.

Frankel, Rachel. "The Couch Tract of the Durham Division of the Duke Forest: A History of Agricultural Land-Use Patterns, 1750-1950." Senior Honors Seminar paper, Duke University, 1984.

Heron, Duncan. "Mill Sites on the Eno River: A Geological Viewpoint." *Eno Journal 7* (1978): 34–40.

Hobbs, Grimsley. *Exploring the Old Mills of North Carolina.* Chapel Hill: Provincial Press, 1985.

Keever, Catherine. "A Retrospective View of Old-Field Succession after 35 Years." *American Midland Naturalist* 110, no. 2 (October 1983): 397–404.

Kenzer, Robert C. *Kinship and Neighborhood in a Southern Community: Orange County, North Carolina, 1849-1881.* Knoxville: University of Tennessee Press, 1987.

King, William E. *If Gargoyles Could Talk: Sketches of Duke University.* Durham: Carolina Academic Press, 1997.

Korstian, C. F. "Report of the Dean of the School of Forestry, 1938–1939." Durham: Duke University, 1940.

———. "Report of the Dean of the School of Forestry, 1939–1940." Durham: Duke University, 1941.

———. "Report of the Director of the Duke Forest, 1932–1933 and 1933–1934." Durham: Duke University, 1935.

———. "Report of the Director of the Duke Forest: 1935–1936." Durham: Duke University, 1937.

———. "Report of the Director of the Duke Forest: 1936–1937." Durham: Duke University, 1938.

Korstian, C. F., and W. Maughan. *The Duke Forest: A Demonstration and Research Laboratory. Duke University Forestry Bulletin*, no. 1. Durham: Duke University, 1931.

Kostyu, Joel A., and Frank A. Kostyu. *Durham: A Pictorial History*. Norfolk: Donning Company Publishers, 1978.

Lefler, Hugh, and Paul Wager, eds. *Orange County, 1752-1952*. Chapel Hill: Orange Printshop, 1953.

Magnuson, Tom. "Some Cultural Resources in the Korstian and Hillsborough Divisions of Duke Forest." Hillsborough: Trading Path Association, 2005.

Maunder, Elwood R. *Clarence F. Korstian: Forty Years of Forestry, An Oral History Interview*. New Haven: Forest History Society, Yale University, 1969.

Miller, Char, and Rebecca Staebler. *The Greatest Good: 100 Years of Forestry in America*. Bethesda: Society of American Foresters, 1999.

Nash, Francis. "The History of Orange County, Part I." *The North Carolina Booklet* 10, no. 2 (October 1910): 56–63.

Oosting, Henry J. "An Ecological History of the Plant Communities of Piedmont, North Carolina." *American Midland Naturalist* 28, no. 1 (July 1942): 1–126.

Patterson, Mann Cabe. *History of the Patterson Family of Orange County, NC 1744-1934*. Chapel Hill: Davie Poplar Chapter, NSDAR, 1934.

Peet, Robert K., and Norman L. Christensen. "Competition and Tree Death." *BioScience* 37, no. 8 (1987): 586–595.

"Preserving Duke Forest." *The New York Times*, November 15, 1987.

Ralston, Charles W. "The Founding Faculty: Some Recollections." *FOREM* 12, no. 1 (1988): 12–16.

Richter, Daniel D., Jr., and Daniel Markewitz. *Understanding Soil Change: Soil Sustainability over Millennia, Centuries, and Decades*. Cambridge: Cambridge University Press, 2001.

Sather, Dawson, and Stephen Hall. Revised edition by Bruce Sorrie and Rich Shaw. *Inventory of Natural Areas and Wildlife Habitats for Orange County, North Carolina*. 1998; Hillsborough: Orange County Environment and Resource Conservation Department, 2004.

Schlesinger, W. H., et. al. "The Duke Forest FACE Experiment: CO_2 Enrichment of a Loblolly Pine Forest." *Ecological Studies* 187 (2006): 197–212.

Shields, Ruth Herndon, Belle Lewter West, and Kathryn Crossley Stone. *A Study of the Barbee Families of Chatham, Orange and Wake Counties in North Carolina*. Boulder: Ruth Herndon Shields, 1971.

Snow, Dan. *In the Company of Stone: The Art of the Stone Wall*. New York: Artisan, 2001.

Steen, Harold K. "Duke's School of Forestry and Environmental Studies at age 50." *FOREM* 12, no. 1 (1988): 5–11.

Taeda: The Yearbook of The School of Forestry, Duke University. Durham: School of Forestry, Duke University, 1963.

Urban Land Institute. "Duke University: An Evaluation of Land Use and Development Strategies for Duke University." Washington, D.C.: Urban Land Institute, 1986.

Vanatta, E. S., L. L. Brinkley, and S. F. Davidson. *Soil Survey of Orange County, North Carolina*. Washington: U.S. Department of Agriculture, 1921.

Wise, Jim. "What's in Store for the Old Store?" Durham News, February 25, 2006, online edition. http://www.rtpnet.org/newhope/news20060225.htm. (accessed February 27, 2006).